Who'll Be in Heaven
&
Who Won't?

Dwight Carlson

A DIVISION OF THOMAS NELSON

WestBow Press books may be ordered through booksellers or by contacting:
WestBow Press
A Division of Thomas Nelson
1663 Liberty Drive
Bloomington, IN 47403
www.westbowpress.com
1-(866) 928-1240

Unless otherwise indicated, all scripture quotations are taken from the
    New King James Version. Copyright 1979, 1980, 1982 by Thomas
    Nelson, inc. Used by permission. All rights reserved.
All scripture quotations marked NET are taken from the New English Translation.
All scripture quotations marked KJV are taken from the King James Version of the Bible.
All scripture quotations marked MSG in this publications are from The Message.
    Copyright (c) by Eugene H. Peterson 1993, 1994, 1995, 1996, 2000,
    2001, 2002. Used by permission of NavPress Publishing Group.
All scripture quotations marked NASB are taken from the New American Standard
    Bible®, Copyright © 1960, 1962, 1963, 1968, 1971, 1972, 1973, 1975, 1977,
    1995 by The Lockman Foundation. Used by permission." (www.Lockman.org)
All scripture quotations marked NIV are taken from the Holy Bible,
    New International Version®. Copyright © 1973, 1978, 1984 Biblica.
    Used by permission of Zondervan. All rights reserved.
All scripture quotations marked RSV are taken from the Revised Standard
    Version of the Bible, copyright 1952 [2nd edition, 1971] by the Division of
    Christian Education of the National Council of the Churches of Christ in
    the United States of America. Used by permission. All rights reserved.
All scripture quotations marked TLB are from The Living
    Bible, by Kenneth N. Taylor, © 1971.

ISBN: 978-1-4497-6627-6 (sc)
ISBN: 978-1-4497-6628-3 (e)
ISBN: 978-1-4497-6629-0 (hc)
Library of Congress Control Number: 2012916256

Printed in the United States of America
WestBow Press rev. date: 3/19/2013

Warning:

This book could be hazardous to your religion—no matter what it is—and change your belief system forever.

Foreword

"Dwight Carlson has courageously tackled some of the toughest questions about heaven/hell and who will and will not be saved. He does it in a way that maintains a high view of biblical authority while acknowledging there are some tough theological questions we will never have fully answered in this life as we "see through a glass darkly." Those who think they have all the answers about how the justice/wrath and mercy/ love of God flesh themselves out will be stopped dead in their tracks by his questioning insights. He avoids the parochialism of being clear on those matters on which the Bible is unclear while maintaining the consistent bedrock understanding that salvation is only through the atoning work of Jesus Christ received by faith not works. Yet he refuses to embrace an antinomianism that dismisses works as irrelevant, calling us to be known by our good works that are the consequences of a redeemed life that desires to obediently follow Jesus Christ as Lord. One cannot read this book and remain content to have easy answers to heavy, complex questions. Instead one is overwhelmed with God's grace coupled with the fact that there are many mysteries that will not be unveiled until "that day." This is a great read for someone willing to let go of the notion of a God who is too small. He leaves room for God to offer his eternal life to those who we have failed to reach with the gospel without a sentimental embrace of non-biblical universalism. Don't read the book unless you are willing to think, have previously unquestioned presuppositions challenged and to consider that perhaps when the veil of mystery is lifted you discover a God more demanding in his righteousness and more mercifully generous in the scope of his salvation than you have previously considered."

Dr. John A. Huffman

Prominent Evangelical figure, chairman of Christianity Today International Board, pastor of St. Andrew's Presbyterian Church in Newport Beach, California, for over 30 years; former chair Board of World Vision; former member, Board of Administration of the National Association of Evangelicals; author of nine books

Other Comments about the Book

"You have done a great service for Christ and His people by writing this book."

Dallas Willard, PhD. Bestselling author and professor at the University of Southern California's School of Philosophy

"Dwight Carlson's *Who'll be in Heaven and Who Won't*, is not about litmus paper tests or who has said the right magic phase to determine where a person will spend eternity. It is about moving beyond easy answers to examine what Scripture has to say on this topic. It is about expanding narrow views to be better able to take in the vastness of God's love. Carlson's writing style is clear and balanced. The reader will see that being "saved" (also read "delivered" or "healed") is about entering into a trusting and interactive relationship with God."

Gary W. Moon, M.Div., Ph.D.

Executive Director Martin Institute and Dallas Willard Center, Westmont College, Author, *Apprenticeship with Jesus*

"Challenging! Calls us to look again at the New Testament understanding of the Church and salvation."

Dr. Paul E. Pierson

Dean Emeritus and Senior Professor of History of Mission and Latin American Studies, School of Intercultural Studies, Fuller Theological Seminary; worldwide lecturer, pastor, and author of five books

"We thank Dr. Carlson for his bold, honest, and scholarly addressing of a very emotionally charged issue. The issue of salvation outside the church is usually only addressed by tenured professors, retired clergy, pastors of large, stable congregations - or independent lay people. It's a topic we all struggle with in our individual hearts, and occasionally in safe company. We thank Dr. Carlson for publicly joining our private conversations. We may not agree, but we are moved."

Rev. Dr. Herbert Hoefer

Missions Chair, Concordia University, Portland, Oregon; missionary and author

"Agree or disagree, my friend Dr. Dwight Carlson makes a significant contribution to the conversation about who can go to heaven. While I don't agree with everything he presents, for a lay leader Dwight has an in-depth biblical worldview and provides a good biblical foundation for the points he makes. You may choose to disagree with his point of view, but this book is well worth reading and comparing to the others currently writing on this important topic. Ultimately, Dwight calls us to examine this matter closely as it is the most important issue we will face someday. He points us to Christ who is the hope of the world and 'the way, the truth and the life.' May you discover Jesus for all that He has to offer through reading this important book!"

Dr. Joe Handley

President of Asian Access

Other key evangelical leaders have personally told me things like "there is no doubt about what you write here" but have been reluctant to have me quote them by name.

**Author of *Overcoming Hurts & Anger*,
over 500,000 copies sold**

Other Books by the Author:

Why Do Christians Shoot Their Wounded?

Overcoming the 7 Obstacles to Spiritual Growth

Energize Your Life

When Life Isn't Fair

From Guilt to Grace

The Will of the Shepherd

Run and Not Be Weary

Dedicated to

My granddaughter, Charissa Wood, with love

Preface

The world is in turmoil, much of it over religious issues: conflict over who is right and who is wrong, who has an edge on God's truth and blessing, ultimately, over who is going to heaven. Consequently, wars are being fought around the world; there is conflict between religions and churches, and yes, individuals themselves are confused on the issue.

J. B. Phillips wrote in *Your God Is Too Small*:

> (To) [t]he Man who is outside all organized Christianity . . . the Churches appear to be saying to him, "you will jump through our particular hoop or sign on our particular dotted line then we will introduce you to God. But if not, then there's no God for you." This seems to him to be nonsense, and nasty arrogant nonsense at that. "If there's a God at all," he feels rather angrily, "then He's here in the home and in the street, here in the pub and in the workshop. And if it's true that He's interested in me and wants me to love and serve Him, then He's available for me and every other Tom, Dick, or Harry, who wants Him, without any interference from the professionals. If God is God, He's *big*, and generous and magnificent, and I can't see that

anybody can say they've made a 'corner' in God, or shut Him up in their particular box." . . . No denomination has a monopoly of God's grace, and none has an exclusive recipe for producing Christian character . . . "the Spirit bloweth where it listeth" and is subject to no regulation of man.[1]

Sitting in a pew week after week, I have had a deep sense that there is a significant body of crucial, spiritual information that is not being discussed or communicated to the average person on the street. Apropos is John Sanders' statement: "I have found that many laypeople have hopes for the unevangelized but do not know how to articulate and defend such hopes. Within evangelicalism, the wider hope is more popular in the pews than in the pulpits."[2] In fact, it has been suggested that religious "leaders have managed to keep a tight lid on this volatile topic."[3]

Terrance L. Tiessen in *Who Can Be Saved?* elaborates further, saying,

There is widespread discomfort among evangelical church members about the teaching that everyone who does not hear the gospel about Jesus will be damned. . . . Back in the 1970's a questionnaire was distributed to students at InterVarsity's conservative student mission convention in Urbana, Illinois. Of the five thousand who replied, only 37 percent believed that a "person who does not hear the gospel is eternally lost," and 25 percent believed that a "man will be saved or lost on the basis of how well he followed what he did know.". . . I think that there is a basic truth that intuitively leads Christians to reject the idea that God would condemn people for not believing in one of whom they have never heard, when only that faith would save them.[4]

It is my opinion that much of the religious world has too narrow a view of God and of who will be saved—and others have far too broad a view of who will go to heaven.[5] Many associated with specific religious groups have a more parochial view of God than is justified. In fact, evangelical/fundamental Christianity has typically communicated that even those who have never had the opportunity of hearing of God's plan of salvation are going to an everlasting fiery inferno, forever and ever, of equal intensity with the Hitlers and mass murders. As a result of these misconceptions, many throw out Christianity, and others in our ranks turn to universalism. I believe both of these conclusions are erroneous.

The aim of this book is to evaluate what the Scriptures actually say on the subject. The goal is to communicate crucial ideas that for the most part are not appreciated by the vast majority of the religious and irreligious alike.

Armed with my own questions, I have now studied a good portion of the literature available, and none of it deals with the subjects quite as I have done, and none of it has altered my conclusions that there is a wider hope than is often communicated to the individual in the pew.

In fact, evangelical/fundamental Christians show tremendous reluctance to openly deal with several of the subjects that this book tackles for fear of where it might lead; but I believe that we, of all individuals, should seek the truth spelled with a small "t" and a capital "T" wherever it leads. Ultimately, I believe that will be most beneficial to all.

This book is the result of being a life-long student of the Bible. My primary desire is to be open to God's truth, wherever that takes me. By profession I am an internist, psychiatrist, and author who has worked with individuals from all walks of life. I am not a professional theologian, but I have tried to live out a life pleasing to God. In researching for a book like this I not only draw from repeatedly reading the Scriptures over the years, but I start the research on a specific subject by reading the Scriptures from cover to cover, marking every verse that might have bearing, as well as considering the overall narrative of the Bible. Then I formulate my ideas from God's Word as his Spirit leads me. Early in my spiritual life I was taught to carefully search the Scriptures and compare passage with passage to come to conclusions regarding God's truth.[6] Not being trained academically as a theologian or philosopher certainly has some disadvantages; but it also has some advantages. The primary source of this book has come from the Scriptures, not other professionals. The Bible teaches that God's Spirit will teach us through his word and that we don't need man's interpretation. Only after my study was completed and most of this book written did I consult man's interpretation of the Scriptures over the last 1,900 years.[7]

This book is written for the average person on the street, in the pew, and yes, in the pub, so technical terms and a detailed evaluation of the pros and cons will be left for the professional theologian.

Richard Mouw, president of Fuller Theological Seminary, quoting in part Japanese theologian Kosuke Koyama, says,

"We all have to decide . . . whether we have a generous God or a stingy God. And the truth is that we evangelicals often give the impression that we have decided to be a spiritually stingy people."[8] Actually it is not my decision or our decision whether we have a generous or stingy God—it's God's. So let's explore his truths together to see if we, in fact, have a generous or stingy God.

This book deals with the most important issue you will ever face in life.

Table of Contents

Chapter 1

You'll Be Surprised by Who Will Be in Heaven

Heathen in Heaven!

About four thousand years ago there was a man of great wealth and high social position, a man who endeavored to worship and serve God to the best of his knowledge even when the stock market crashed to zero and he lost his health, wealth, and children.[1]

His friends turned against him, and his critical wife advised him to curse God and die. His actual knowledge about God appears very limited. As far as we know he had no contact with any organized religion on the earth. Based on when in history he probably lived, he never heard of Jehovah of the Old Testament, and he lived long before Christ or Mohammed walked the face of the earth. For all intents and purposes, he was a heathen attempting to the best of his knowledge and ability to worship God—whoever he was. Yet I doubt whether any Jew, Christian, or Muslim would question Job's being in heaven. The question is how, on what basis, was he saved? His wife and his religious friends had a lot of good religious advice for him, but Job stuck to his guns and in due time God vindicated him. I have absolutely no doubt that I will see him in heaven, as the Scriptures say, "for the LORD had accepted Job."[2]

Other Jobs?

Let's put it another way: do you think there is any possibility that throughout all the earth, down through the ages, there *could* be another very righteous man who loved, obeyed, and feared God despite a very imperfect knowledge of the Almighty—we might refer to him as Job II? I think we are forced to say there certainly *could be*. How about a Job III? Is it even possible in some remote jungle today there is a Job IV? Again, I believe, the answer has to be *yes*.[3]

Furthermore, there will be many other unexpected people in heaven, such as the lying prostitute Rahab[4] and the wicked Ninevites who turned from their sin to worship the living Creator. Theirs was an evil civilization; the Israelites hated them, and the Hebrew prophet Jonah resisted God's desire that he urge them to repent. After much arm-twisting by God, Jonah finally went to Nineveh, and to his dismay, they listened to God's message and repented in sackcloth and ashes. I'll see them in heaven.[5]

Of course there will be many whom most of us would expect to be in heaven, such as Adam and Eve's son Abel, who offered an appropriate offering and was killed by his jealous brother.[6] Most would agree that the stalwarts in the early days of Judaism—such as Noah,[7] Abraham, and Moses—will be in heaven.

I'm sure we'll see the first Christians ever—the Persian magi, from either the current Iraq or Iran, who were priests, wise men, and of all things, *astrologers*, following by faith a strange and miraculous leading.[8] Of course the thief who was crucified with Christ and was told by Jesus that "today you will be with Me in Paradise" will certainly be saved.[9] The Roman centurion to whom Christ said, "I have not found such great faith not even in Israel," will be there.[10] Then there will be the black treasurer from Ethiopia who was seeking to worship the true God and so went to Jerusalem and on the way home was enlightened.[11]

The Hebrew disciple Peter struggled with repulsion at God's beckoning him to go to the Gentile Cornelius and teach him about God's truths. He ultimately concluded: "I perceive that God shows no partiality, but in every nation whoever fears [God] and works righteousness *is* accepted by Him."[12] I could greatly expand on this list; but I believe you get the point. This roster spans many different nationalities over thousands of years and many miles, all enjoying the benefits of heaven.

Thus, I surmise that individuals will be in heaven who have never been part of any organized religion, individuals who respond to God's grace and will enter the pearly gates. Such a conclusion is crucial; otherwise many people in the world who have never had the opportunity to hear about the true God could never enter heaven. That would not be fair—and I believe God is both fair and just. Rhetorically, the Scriptures say, "shall not the God of all the earth do right?"[13] I assert he has and always will do what is right. This addresses the most frequently asked question about Christianity on college campuses today.[14]

C. S. Lewis poignantly articulates the dilemma that most of us struggle with:

> Here is another thing that used to puzzle me. Is it not frightfully unfair that this new [Christian] life should be confined to people who have heard of Christ and been able to believe in Him? But the truth is God has not told us what His arrangements about the other people are. We do know that no man can be saved except through Christ; we do not know that only those who know Him can be saved through Him.[15]

The highly respected theologian J. I. Packer elaborates further saying:

> We may say (i) if any good pagan reached the point of throwing himself on his Maker's mercy for pardon, it was grace that brought him there; (ii) God will surely save anyone he brings thus far (*cf.* Acts 10:34f.; Rom. 10:12f.); (iii) anyone thus saved would learn in the next world that he was saved through Christ. But what we cannot safely say is that God ever does save anyone this way.[16]

The British theologian Alister E. McGrath takes it a step further:

> God's revelation is not limited to the explicit human preaching of the good news, but extends beyond it. We must be prepared to be surprised at those whom we will meet in the kingdom of God. In his preaching of the good news of the kingdom, Jesus lists some who will be among its beneficiaries—

the Ninevites, the queen of Sheba, and those who lived in the cities of Tyre, Sidon, Sodom, and Gomorrah. . . . By strict Jewish standards none of these had any claim to be in the kingdom of God. Yet God's mercy extended far beyond the human limits devised by this rather narrow-minded section of Judaism. *Perhaps there is a danger that today's Christians will repeat this mistake, even with the best of intentions, by placing artificial human limits on the sovereignty, freedom, and love of God.*[17]

On What Basis Will These Individuals Be Saved?

But what is the basis on which people outside of traditional Christianity are saved? On what basis might they go to heaven? What is the common denominator—if there is one? In studying the Scriptures I believe a prerequisite is that *God causes* the individual to be profoundly aware of his or her personal need— of his or her self-centered life—and then that person turns towards God. This motivates one to move toward the next two requirements. As Peter concludes after his vision, "I perceive that God shows no partiality, but in every nation whoever *fears Him [believes in, trusts God]* and *works righteousness* is accepted by Him."[18] We need to have a deep faith or trust in God, which will inevitably lead to *a life and conduct that will exemplify such a faith.*[19]

Fleshing out these ideas more specifically, an individual must (1) be aware of his or her personal need—that one doesn't measure up to God's righteous standards;[20] (2) respond to God's prompting;[21] (3) have a deep belief in a sovereign God and worship him only;[22] (4) repent;[23] and as a result, (5) lead a life that demonstrates evidence of that faith in a righteous God.[24] These points will be elaborated in greater detail later.

God's Concern for the World

In the Old Testament it seems as though God favors the Jews over all other people, and there is no question that God has a special love for them. But we must remember that the Old Testament is told through the eyes of Hebrew prophets. Yet even so, numerous passages describe God's great concern, not only for the Jews, but for all the people of the world. *God has always been concerned about the peoples of the entire world.*[25]

In the second book of the Bible, referring to Moses, God says, "But indeed for this purpose I have raised you up, that I may show My power in you, and that My name may be declared in all the earth." To Abraham God stated, "I will bless you . . . *and all peoples on earth will be blessed through you.*"[26]

Let's look at a few select verses *in just one book* in the Old Testament, the book of Psalms:

> The LORD is near to those who have a broken heart.
> And [He] saves such as have a contrite spirit.[27]
> The sacrifices of God are a broken spirit.
> A broken and a contrite heart—
> These, O God, You will not despise.[28]
> That Your way may be known on earth,
> Your salvation among *all* nations. . . .
> For You shall judge the people righteously. . . .
> And *all* the ends of the earth shall fear Him.[29]

And none of those who trust in Him shall be
   condemned.[30]
For You, Lord, are good, and ready to forgive.
   And abundant in mercy to *all* those who call
   upon You.[31]

Christ makes it exceedingly clear that God's concern encompasses the entire world and that there will be those from "other folds" hearing his voice.[32] The entire Bible teaches that "those who seek me diligently will find me" and "that *whoever* calls on the name of the LORD shall be saved"[33]

There Will Be Saved Individuals Out of Every Tribe, Tongue, and Nation

The Scriptures state there will be individuals from every tribe, language group, and nation in heaven.[34] It is commendable that many are working hard to reach every people group with God's good news, a topic we will address later. I have been a financial supporter of this work for years. But there have been tribes and tongues that no longer exist, many before the time Christ walked on the earth.[35] So how can there be "saved" ones in heaven from these people groups unless there are Job-like people among them? There may not be many—but I would suggest that individuals with a Job-like faith and life certainly could be the answer.

The Scriptures say that "God looks down from heaven upon the children of men, to see if there are any who understand, who seek [Him]" and that he "is a rewarder of those who diligently seek him."[36] In fact, it is God's ultimate desire for all to "be saved and to come to the knowledge of the truth."[37]

Furthermore, God judges individuals according to the knowledge given them.[38] Many theologians hold to such a position, as stated by Dr. Michael Licona, professor of philosophy at Southwestern Baptist Theological Seminary: *"God will judge us according to our response to the knowledge we received."*[39]

A Parochial View of Who's Going to Heaven

If you deny the possibility of there being other people like Job—that is, other "heathen" who truly worship God to the extent of their knowledge about God and live a life manifesting such faith—then you have made God into a parochial god, one who favors you and your stripe of religiosity and no one else's. You have also—it seems to me—made God into an unjust god. For if a person could live and not have the possibility of going to heaven—and be condemned to eternal damnation—then it seems to me that God would be unfair. That is not the God I worship, nor do I believe it is the God of the universe. We have a very gracious God who does not desire that any should perish.

It is very possible that there will be many "non-Christians" in heaven, people who have never been part of an organized religious group—people who have never heard the name of Abraham, Moses, or Jesus Christ.[40] Even Christ said, "other sheep I have, which are not of this fold."[41] They also will have eternal life.

A giant problem of virtually all religions is their parochial view of *"their"* God. *God's on our team and all the rest of you are out*, in fact, *going straight to hell*. Some of us need a broader view of our great God, as did the Jews and early Christians. Virtually *all* religious groups struggle with this attitude of religious superiority—and it persists today. William Barclay has said, "The greatest of all heresies is the sinful conviction that any Church has a monopoly of God or of his truth, or that any Church is the only gateway to God's Kingdom."[42] Peter had great difficulty realizing God accepted individuals who had a deep faith in him and lived a life consistent with that faith if they weren't in the exact spiritual and cultural mold he was in and therefore thought they should be in.[43]

Who Is "In" and Who Is "Out"?

Down through the ages religious groups have always been narrow minded over whom they think is "in" and "out," that is, who is going to heaven and who is not.

For example, the Jewish people have been and are special to God. But often they have responded with elitism. Some followers of Moses wanted to censure other individuals who were clearly blessed by God but weren't in the "in group." Moses refused.[44] The Jewish people hated the heathen Ninevites, and Jonah, a Jew, resisted for a time God's direct command to take the good news of God's grace to them. Jonah even got depressed when the Ninevites responded to God's calling them to repent. The prophet Elijah was convinced that he was the only faithful God-fearer around until he was informed that there were 7,000 others nearby.[45]

The Jewish religious leaders of Christ's day certainly didn't think he was part of the "in group." Christ's disciples were often guilty of the same thing. As they viewed themselves as the "in group," they wanted Christ to censor little children or a Palestinian woman. Another time they pleaded with Christ to condemn some followers of his actual teachings but who were not in lockstep with them—in each case Christ blatantly refused.[46]

Later, the leader of the church had to be pushed to acknowledge God's love and grace to those defiled, "heathen" Gentiles. Peter finally came to the conclusion that "God shows no partiality. But in every nation whoever *fears Him and works righteousness is* accepted by Him."[47]

The early church held to many of the Jewish customs and had tremendous difficulty believing that individuals could be "in" who they thought were "out"; that they could be accepted by God without following the Old Testament rules and culture. These disciples were called "Judaizers." They wanted to make every Christian fit their Jewish brand of Christianity, holding on to many of their traditions and practices. They wanted everyone to convert and become a cultural and religious Jew *in order* to meet Jesus, but God's Spirit did an end-run and led Gentiles to meet Jesus without changing cultures or becoming Jews. Even the Elder John was confronted with this in-vs.-out problem created by some self-serving local church leaders.[48] By such standards most of us would be "out" of God's grace today.

God frequently steps outside the box and accepts people we don't think should be "in," that is, accepted by God and going to heaven. Scripture from beginning to end invites into the kingdom of God people that the established religious organization of the day thinks should be kept out, and Scripture likewise rejects some they think should be let in. We are no different today. My wife, who was raised in a very strict legalistic Christianity, was shocked to discover in nurses' training that Presbyterians might be Christians. I suspect many of us are going to be shocked by whom we find in heaven—and who is missing![49]

Even Luther said there will be surprises in heaven. Later we will focus on some who won't be there; but for now let's focus on the many who will be there.

If we aren't careful we can easily become the self-righteous elder brother who judges everyone else and ends up with a plank in our eyes while judging people with only a speck in theirs.[50] God is much bigger than that, not limiting himself to any one group of people, whether ethnic or religious. He always has been and remains concerned for every person in the world. "God loves every person in the world and does not desire any to perish."[51]

Roman Catholics in Heaven

As a Protestant, naturally, I believe that many Protestants will be in heaven—but likewise, many won't. We will get into that later. When I grew up though, Roman Catholics were anathema; I knew very little about them at the time except for their fund-raising bazaars, emphasis on works, history of inquisitions, burning people at the stake, and keeping the Scriptures from the common person. They certainly weren't the "in group" among the people I was around. In fact, they were one of the "out groups." As I have grown, hopefully, a little more mature, I have learned to know wonderful Catholics with a deep trust in Christ and a life consistent with that faith, and I am confident many will be in heaven. In fact, as I read about the life and faith of Mother Teresa of Calcutta, I differ with a lot of her theology—but you know, I believe she is going to be a long way in front of me in heaven.[52]

Mormons in Heaven

Then there are Mormons—members of the Church of Jesus Christ of Latter-day Saints. For years I associated them with two young men in white shirts and ties riding bikes and knocking on your door to get into dialogue with you and hopefully convert you. For years I really didn't know any Mormons nor had I investigated what they believed. Sure, I think they add many unnecessary things to the Scriptures—*but what organized religious group doesn't?*[53]

There are many things not stated or that are ambiguous in the Scriptures about which every religious faction gets uncomfortable; thus they want to clarify or define the issue or doctrine for themselves and their followers. Then they will have a basis to determine who is "in" and who is "out," who they, and everybody else, should allow in their group and endorse as going to heaven, and who is, in fact, a heretic.

Mormons hold that baptism is necessary for salvation—but then, some evangelical groups emphasize it to the point that it seems necessary to be a Christian. To this day I have never heard a good explanation for how the thief on the cross was guaranteed heaven though was never baptized.[54] Mormons forbid not only alcohol and cigarettes but also caffeine. When I grew up I was taught that lipstick and dancing were sin, as were pictures that moved—now called motion pictures or movies. All religions include those who rely on their supposed good life/works to get them into heaven—and if that is their basis for entry they are going to be greatly disappointed. Mormons are particularly at risk with their strong emphases on a moral life, good works, legalism, temple ritual, and extra-biblical books. We will have more to say about this in later chapters.

However, as I have gotten to know Mormons, my opinion about them has changed. I have some relatives who are Mormons—dear, wonderful people—who clearly have a deep faith in the finished work of Christ and live exemplary lives. I anticipate seeing them in heaven.

Robert L. Millet, a Mormon scholar, says in *A Different Jesus? The Christ of the Latter-Day Saints*:

> Jesus Christ is the central figure in the doctrine and practice of The Church of Jesus Christ of Latter-day Saints. . . . Jesus explained that "no man cometh unto the Father, but by me" (John 14:6). Latter-day Saints acknowledge Jesus Christ as the source of truth and redemption, as the light and life of the world, as the way to the Father.[55]

Regarding baptism, which Mormons strongly emphasize, he says: "while baptism or other ordinances are necessary as channels of divine power and grace, they are not the things that save us. *Jesus* saves us!"

Millet goes on to say that while he was discussing these issues, a friend turned to him one day and asked:

> Okay Bob, here's the question of questions; there is one thing I would like to ask in order to determine what you really believe: You are standing before the judgment bar of the Almighty, and God turns to you and asks: "Robert Millet, what right do you have to enter heaven? Why should I let you in?"
>
> He replies: "I would say to God: I claim the right to enter heaven because of my complete trust

in and reliance upon the merits and mercy and grace of the Lord Jesus Christ."[56]

Gordon B. Hinckley, fifteenth president of the LDS Church was asked, "Are we Christians?" His response was, "Of course we are! . . . no one believes more literally in the redemption wrought by the Lord Jesus Christ. No one believes more fundamentally that He was the Son of God, that He died for the sins of mankind, that He arose from the grave, and that He is the living resurrected Son of the living Father."[57]

Richard Mouw, recent president and professor of Christian philosophy at Fuller Theological Seminary, is an individual who has gone to great efforts to heal the fractured relationships that have existed between the Mormons and evangelical Christians. In the afterword endorsing Robert Millet's book, he says, *"I also know that having a genuine personal relationship with Jesus Christ does not require that we have all our theology straight. All true Christians are on a journey, and until we see the Savior face-to-face we will all see through a glass darkly."*[58] I couldn't say a heartier "Amen" to that.

Chapter 2

Muslims, Hindus, and Buddhists in Heaven?

Bilquis, a Pakistani Muslim, tells her miraculous story in *I Dared to Call Him Father*.[1] She initially had turned to the Qur'an, but in a strange way was drawn to read the Bible. She had repeated dreams reaffirming what she was reading in the New Testament. She had a sense of *Presence* as she dreamed about the prophet Isa (Jesus). She was urged to talk to God as her Father, which was a totally new experience for her. Ultimately, she became outspoken in her faith at great risk to her life. To her advantage she had been in a position of stature in the community, which protected her for awhile. She was led to help others to faith, telling them if they wanted to know this Jesus they would just have to ask him to come into their hearts. But eventually even she had to flee for her life to a "Christian" country.

If you lived in a predominantly Muslim country such as Saudi Arabia or Iran and found a New Testament or turned on your somewhat camouflaged satellite TV to a Christian broadcast and had an encounter with Christ—what would you do?

You could try and get a visa and emigrate to a "Christian" nation, forsake your family and culture, and take on a Western-Christian culture. In so doing you would lose any witness in your community.

What if you couldn't get a visa and/or wanted to remain in your country of birth and witness to your family and friends? You basically would have two options. You could announce to your community that you have become a Christian, try and find someone to baptize you, and look for a Christian fellowship. A likely scenario is that within a week or two your father, brother, or uncle would pay you a visit late one evening with a knife in his belt and authorities would turn a blind eye as you bled to death.[2]

But there is another option that many thousands of Muslims, Hindus, Buddhists, and even Jews are utilizing—you could become part of a "Jesus Movement" or "Insider Movement."[3] Paul E. Pierson, Senior Professor of History of Mission and Latin American Studies at Fuller Theological Seminary, says, "In Acts 15 clearly the Church . . . is being released from its Jewish forms to take on new forms in gentile culture. Could it be that today, the People of God is being released from its western, Christendom forms to find new forms in non-western, non Christendom cultures?"[4]

An article titled "Muslim Followers of Jesus?" in *Christianity Today* asks, "Can one be Muslim and a follower of Jesus? Tens of thousands believe so." Just as there are Messianic Jews, the article says that in the 1980s a similar movement began among Muslims who had come to faith in Christ—Muslim followers of Jesus. They have been referred to as "Messianic Muslims," authentic disciples of Christ who want to remain within their Muslim culture, honoring Jesus in that context. It describes Muslim-background believers in Christ-centered communities (for short referred to as "Cs") by categorizing them in six different groups on a scale of 1 through 6: "C1s" are believers in Christ who take on a lifestyle and worship closely aligned to Western Christians. At the other end of the spectrum are the "C6s" who are secret believers in Jesus. The article concludes: "we must respect [the Muslim believers'] fundamental human right to sort out—under the authority of Scripture—how they express their identity as followers of Christ. It is they whose lives are quite literally on the line."[5]

If I were a Muslim believer in Christ in a strongly Muslim country—right or wrong—I'm not sure how outspoken I would be about my faith. I suspect I would hold on to my faith but try to do so unnoticed to avoid being killed for being a follower of the Messiah. Even Peter, the rock of the church, cursed as he denied he knew Christ in a pivotal moment of Christ's and Peter's lives.[6] Rahab wasn't condemned for lying to save her own skin and the Jews she was hiding.[7] Christ didn't criticize the secret follower Nicodemus. Nor was the Syrian Naaman criticized having a saving faith and even was given permission by the prophet Elisha to bow himself in the heathen temple as was expected by his culture.[8]

Muslim believers are becoming aware that they can follow Christ without giving up their culture. Mazhar Mallouhi is a Syrian who became a follower of Christ indirectly through Mahatma Gandhi, who in turn was profoundly influenced by Jesus. In one year Mazhar read the Old Testament thirteen times and the New Testament twenty-seven times and his life was transformed.[9] "When Mazhar became a follower of Christ, Arab Christians told him that he needed to leave his cultural past behind so he dislocated himself from his Islamic way of life (family, community, etc.) and attempted to take on a 'Christian culture.'" They even wanted him to eat pork and embrace Zionism. Mazhar eventually came to the conclusion that *he could hold to his cultural past and still be a disciple of Christ*. He calls himself a "Muslim follower of Christ," and he says, "Islam is my heritage. Christ is my inheritance."[10]

In fact, it is said that a revolution is going on and not just against the West. One Internet ministry to Muslims indicates hundreds if not thousands are making decisions for Christ every day.[11] In Iran, seventy percent of the population is watching Christian satellite programs. Surveys suggest that at least one million have become followers of Jesus.[12] New Testaments translated with an understanding of Muslim culture are highly sought after. "There are even imams in places like East Africa who preach from the Bible in their mosques. God appears to be working across the board."[13] I think we must be careful about being "Christian Judaizers," imposing our Christian traditions, many of which are extra-biblical, and Western culture, much of which is nonbiblical, on Muslim believers.

Some would, out of hand, dismiss all of this, saying, "Muslims worship a different god." I think we must be very careful here. Do Christians worship a different God than Abraham did? He would have described Yahweh very differently than would a Christian theologian today—but I maintain they are worshiping the same God.[14] What about Pentecostals and

Presbyterians—do they worship a different God? I don't think so, even though some of their doctrine is different. You might quickly object, saying the difference between two Protestant denominations and two different religions can't be compared— and I would agree. But I also have to caution that you and I don't know what is in a person's heart. Peter was offended that Cornelius's culture and religious practices didn't jive with his. But God saw Cornelius's heart. Remember: "the LORD does not see as man sees; for man looks at the outward appearance, but the LORD looks at the heart."[15] Furthermore, "the eyes of the Lord search back and forth across the whole earth, looking for people whose hearts are perfect toward him, so that he can show his great power in helping them."[16] God wants to and will reveal himself to individuals whose hearts are open to him.

Lets look at it another way. When Christ cried out on the cross "My God, My God, why have You forsaken Me?" he cried out: My *"Alahi,"* My *"Alahi,"* why have You forsaken Me? For *Alahi* is the Aramaic word for God. In fact, the word *Allah* was used by Arab Christians before Muhammad's time, and it is still used today. Christians in the Arab world—even as you read this—pray to Allah every day. They're praying to God. When any true believer prays in Arabic, God *is* Allah, and Allah *is* God. Moreover, every translation of the Bible into Arabic uses the word *Allah* for *God.*[17]

I am not contending that *all* "Muslims" are praying to the "right God" any more than I would contend that *all* "Christians" are praying to the "right God." Remember, the Lord looks at the heart. I suspect the heart of the individual is far more important to God than anything else.

Mark D. Siljander, who served in the U.S. Congress and later as alternate representative to the United Nations General Assembly, describes in *A Deadly Misunderstanding* an incident when he was addressing 150 Christian missionaries and doctors of theology who were expecting him to say, in essence, "Islam is of the devil." Instead he asked them if they minded if he opened with a few passages from Scripture. They indicated: "Please do!" So he read:

> Jesus is the Messiah . . . sinless, supernaturally conceived through a virgin named Mary by the spirit of God, was taken up to be close to God and will be the judge of the world. . . . He is the Word of God, He is the Word of Truth. . . . He heals the sick and the blind, He can even raise the dead.

> Everyone in the audience was listening in rapt attention, nodding their heads, some calling out "Hallelujah!" and "Praise the Lord!" Then [he] stopped and looked up at them [and said] Every word I just spoke came from the Qur'an."[18]

I think we must be very careful about passing judgment too quickly on Muslim believers in Christ.

Visions and Dreams?

I don't know about you, but I get uncomfortable with any talk about supernatural encounters from God. Maybe it is from some of the excesses I saw in the 1960s, or maybe it's my psychiatric training and experience. But they clearly happen in the Scriptures. Numerous and diverse supernatural encounters appear in both the Old and New Testaments.[19] Could that be happening today?

In fact, hearing some of the things being reported, we have to perk up our ears and wonder if we are seeing prophecy's fulfillment before our eyes where it says: "it shall come to pass in the last days, says God, That I will pour out My Spirit on all flesh; Your sons and your daughters . . . shall see visions, Your old men shall dream dreams. . . . I will pour out My Spirit in those days."[20] Particularly in "closed countries," there are reports of individuals having all sorts of visions and dreams, suggesting that God is reaching out to those hungry for the truth. A recent account says:

> [I]t is now common knowledge that a small but growing number of Afghan believers reside within their communities. . . . Stories abound in Afghanistan about meeting the Lord in a dream or vision. Some workers have begun to ask Afghans, "Have you ever had a dream about a man in white?" as a way to open a conversation. A young man in Eastern Afghanistan, Najib, tells this story: "I had a copy of the Injil (New Testament) and had read parts of it. One morning I awoke early and went to the forest for a walk in the cool part of the day. On my walk I was met by Isa Masi (Jesus). I was so amazed! The next day I got up early to see if we could meet again. Yes, He was there! I was afraid to tell anyone because I thought He might not come back. Every day for three months I walked with Him in this forest."[21]

Reports like this are common, and it is crucial that we are open to God using such encounters today. As God directed the Persian magi (the very first seekers who found Jesus through a miraculous means), it appears that even today God is using visions and dreams among many Muslim seekers. In *Who Can Be Saved?* Terrance L. Tiessen states:

> J. Dudley Woodbery and Russell Shubin report the findings of their ten-year study of about six hundred Muslim-background believers, and they comment: "For someone who has not had extended exposure to Muslim-background believers in Christ, probably the most striking surprise is the powerful role that dreams and visions have played in drawing people to Jesus." Rick Love, international director of Frontiers, a missions organization, writes, "Just as God used a vision to convert Paul, in like manner He reveals Himself to Muslims through dreams and visions. Just as God prepared Cornelius to hear the Gospel through a vision, so God is preparing a multitude of Muslims to respond to His good news."[22]

Visions and dreams are not just limited to Muslim countries. Tissani of India says, "I had a dream. . . . Jesus came in a dream and said to me, 'Don't worry, I will make your [lower caste people be educated]. She came to believe there is one God, Jesus, whom she seeks to follow."[23]

The apostle Paul wrote: "There is no longer Jew or Gentile . . . you are one in Christ Jesus." I wonder if he were writing today he would say "There is no longer Jew, Gentile, or Muslim . . .

you are one in Christ Jesus."[24] Culture doesn't matter; what is crucial is believing in Isa (Jesus).

Buddhists and Hindus Saved?

Recently I heard a Christian Japanese professor who taught in Japan for many years say that he is aware of a thousand Buddhists who, he believes, are saved. Unfortunately, I have not been able to verify this statement. However, the book *Churchless Christianity* describes research in southern India, where there are hundreds of thousands of Hindu and Muslim believers in Christ who, due to their society's alienation of Christians, do not discard their Hindu or Muslim culture and likewise do not fully identify with believers in Christ. There are significant social, economic, and political consequences of being a baptized Christian.[25] It marks them and alienates them from their culture; it affects their chances of marriage and owning property. It interferes with getting scholarships, business rights, and employment. They may even be restricted from using the village well and denied health care. Young people become secret followers to avoid being sent out of their house and losing all social and economic security in life.

In 1925, the phenomenal missionary to India, E. Stanley Jones, wrote:

> This whole chapter might be summed up in the statement of the Brahman [a member of the highest caste and a priest among Hindus] who put his hand on my shoulder (and I am untouchable!) and said, "Sir, you perhaps become discouraged at the few who become Christians from the high castes. You

need not be discouraged. You do not know how far your gospel has gone. Now, look at me, I am a Brahman, but I would call myself a Christian Brahman, for I am trying to live my life upon the principles and spirit of Jesus, though I may never come out and be an open follower of Jesus Christ, but I am following him. Sir, don't be discouraged, you do not know how far your gospel has gone."[26]

Some postulate that such followers of Christ are more effective witnesses staying within the Hindu culture. They say, "my faith is in Christ. Outside I am a Hindu, but inside I am a Christian." They take part in religious-cultural festivals and even stand before an idol, but pray to Jesus. In one home there is a large picture of Hindu gods in the main room, but in the room where the owner worships there is only a picture of Jesus.[27] *Churchless Christianity* goes on to say:

It would be fair, then, to say that a good one-third of the Madras City population relate to Jesus fairly regularly and fairly deeply in their spiritual life. . . . By now it can come as no surprise that there are true believers in Jesus Christ among the Hindu and Muslim population of Madras City. . . .[28]

One missionary in Sri Lanka told about a group of Buddhist converts who were meeting for the last time before they would together take baptism the next day. One of the members of the group told with joy how he planned to go to the Buddhist temple that evening for one last time. . . . [He wanted] to say thanks to God for all [he had] received through being a Buddhist. He felt *that he had been led through the goodness of Buddhism to seek the Source of all goodness in Christ,* and for that he could only be thankful.[29]

I believe God's Spirit was seeing his heart, pursuing him, and using whatever was at his disposal to draw this Buddhist to Christ.

Muslim, Hindu, and Buddhist Followers of Jesus

In an editorial comment by Rick Wood, editor of *Mission Frontiers*, titled "Muslim, Hindu and Buddhist Followers of Jesus: How Should We Respond?" says that "[i]t is also hard for many of us—especially those in the West—to fathom how someone can remain a 'Muslim' or 'Hindu' and still faithfully follow Jesus from a solidly biblical foundation. . . . It is what is in the heart that counts, not what can be seen on the outside."[30] In the same issue Gavriel Gefen writes about "Jesus Movements":

> There is a growing phenomenon taking place concurrently within at least every sizeable region of the world today. People within numerous different tribal cultures and also people within the cultures of each of the major world religions are increasingly accepting Jesus without converting to Christianity and without joining churches. They are learning to discover for themselves what it means to be faithful to Jesus within their own cultures and within their own birth communities. Conversion for them is believed to be a matter of the heart and not one of joining a different, competing culture

community. . . . It becomes a Jesus movement within another tradition. . . . How did Jesus live as a son of Israel? Did he create a separate and competing community from the one that was already there? Did he tell people to leave their synagogues? Did he start his own synagogues? Didn't he seek to bring transformation and new life to the community that was already there?

The first followers of Jesus did not leave their synagogues. They began meeting regularly in small groups for fellowship, study, and prayer centered around Jesus while remaining part of the synagogues they were already in.[31]

This same article goes on to say:

Jews in Israel today finally have the conditions necessary to be able once again to confidently and wholeheartedly accept Jesus as Israel's Messiah while remaining firmly within the traditional synagogue community.

This is not a reference to what is called Messianic Jewish movement. This is referring to a growing phenomenon of Jews following Jesus within Judaism. Increasing numbers of Jews are learning to follow Jesus faithfully within their traditional synagogue communities.[32]

Many call themselves "a Jewish Israeli who follows Jesus." Movements to Jesus are springing up among Muslims, Hindus, Buddhists and many other cultures of the world. When these peoples accept the fullness of who Jesus really is and then learn to faithfully follow him while remaining socially and culturally within their own communities, they do a similar thing to what Jewish followers of Jesus are beginning to do in Israel once again.[33]

These "Jesus Movements" or "insider groups" are springing up not only within the Jewish culture, but also Muslim, Hindu, and Buddhist cultures.[34] The early followers of Christ went to the synagogue on Saturday, believed it was essential to practice circumcision and avoid pork, but then worshiped Christ in their homes on Sundays. It was extremely difficult for Peter and many others to realize that one could be a true believer apart from these cultural badges of "true belief." It is equally difficult for us "Christians" to recognize that a Muslim can avoid pork, fast, heed the call to worship five times a day, go to the mosque on Friday, pray on a prayer mat to Isa (Jesus) and be "saved." But this is happening not only among Muslims but many other religious groups.

Whom Does God Hear?

Dallas Willard, in *The Divine Conspiracy*, writes:

> Do Jesus and his Father hear Buddhists when they call upon them? They hear *anyone* who calls upon them. "The Lord is near to the brokenhearted, and saves those who are crushed in spirit.". . . There is no distinction between 'Jew and Greek,' between those who have "it"—however humans may define "it"—and those who do not, "for the same one is Lord of all, abounding in riches to all who call upon

him.". . . . You cannot call upon Jesus Christ or upon God and *not* be heard. . . . he continues to speak in ways that serious inquirers can hear if they will.[35]

Hudson Taylor was an unparalleled missionary to China in the middle of the nineteenth century who left everything in England at a tremendous cost personally and to his family. Though criticized by other foreigners, he adopted the Chinese dress of the day: shaving the front part of his head and letting his hair grow into a regulation queue (pigtail). He had a burning desire to tell people how they could be saved. One day, Mr. Ni, a Buddhist leader, heard that Mr. Taylor was speaking about religious issues, which were of great concern to him. After he heard Mr. Taylor speak, he said to him, "I have long sought the Truth, but without finding it. I have traveled far and near, but have never searched it out. In Confucianism, Buddhism, Taoism, I have found no rest. But I do find rest in what we have heard tonight. Henceforth, I am a believer."[36]

"He became an ardent student of the Bible and his growth in knowledge and grace was wonderful." However, when he heard that the missionaries had had God's "Truth" for hundreds of years, he responded, "'What! Hundreds of years?' 'My father sought the Truth,' he continued sadly, 'and died without finding it. Oh, why did you not come sooner?' It was a moment, the pain of which Hudson Taylor could never forget.'"[37]

Hudson Taylor is another one who is going to be so far in front of me in heaven that I won't even see the back of his queue.[38] Nevertheless, I think if I were responding to Mr. Ni, I would ask, "Did your father have the same kind of faith that you had before you heard Mr. Taylor speak, and do you think he would have responded as readily to the Truth as you did?" If Mr. Ni answered affirmatively, I think I would tell him, "You know, I can't be absolutely sure, but I suspect that your father is in heaven right now and will welcome you when you arrive." You might ask: "On what basis would I say this?" First of all, I think it is consistent with the points that I am making in this book. Furthermore, I believe I have as much of a basis as religious leaders of virtually all stripes who immediately console the grieving parents of an infant or young child who has died, saying that he or she is in heaven with absolutely no scriptural basis for such a conclusion. I am not arguing against such a position, but I believe one can make an equal if not much stronger case for individuals like Mr. Ni's father being in heaven and consoling Mr. Ni.

Edith Schaeffer, cofounder of L'Abri Fellowship, tells the story of a man named Honey II, of the Lisu tribe from the remote hills of China. "He had known nothing but heathen teaching all his life, but was 'seeking'" God, and he found a scrap of a page torn from a catechism that said, "Are there more gods than One?" and answered it, "No, there is only One God." It went on to ask: "Should we worship idols?" And the torn page answered: "No." As a result of only this information he went home and "tore down his demon altars," and immediately his daughter became deathly ill. Neighbors taunted him that he had made the demons angry. Not knowing what to do, he climbed the highest mountain peak—some 12-14,000 feet high—in hopes that he could reach God. There he cried out, "Oh, God, if You really are there and You are the One I am to worship, please make my little girl well again." When he finally arrived back at his hut, his daughter was well. The time of her healing was exactly when he cried out to God.[39] Edith Schaeffer goes on to say:

> God has promised: *If with all thine heart ye truly seek Me, ye shall surely find Me.* . . . God is gentle and tender with the truly honest and seeking hearts. . . . There will be so many stories to compare with Honey II's that I picture us taking thousands of years to find out about them all. The compassion and the tenderness of our loving Heavenly Father will take forever to learn about.[40]

In fact, Christ indicates that there are going to be a lot of individuals who are very surprised by both who will be in heaven and who won't be in heaven.[41] We will see individuals in heaven from every tribe, tongue, and nation—including some who might disagree with me theologically. I suspect there will be some to whom I would be prone to say: "What are you doing here?" and they might be prone to say the same to me.

But that's only half the story—let's take a look at the other half.

Chapter 3

You'll Be Surprised by Who Won't Be in Heaven

Before we get carried away with the inclusiveness of God's love and grace towards humankind, we need to pause and look at the other side of the picture. It appears that there are a lot of people who think they'll be in heaven—who won't be.

I have some very good friends who are universalists; they maintain that everyone will go to heaven. I must respectfully disagree. I believe Satan often causes humans to react to an extreme position with an opposite extreme. As a reaction to hell being a literal burning in lava forever, I believe many have gone to the other extreme, universalism: the notion that everyone will ultimately go to heaven. I do not believe the Scriptures contain any credible evidence for the position that everyone will eventually be saved. I have one friend who says, "Hitler will be in heaven." I hope I don't offend him, but I don't see how a just God cannot require recompense from the Hitlers, the Stalins, the Pol Pots, and the Idi Amins of the world.[1] More importantly, the Scriptures speak of some terrible consequences for individuals like that. The Scriptures say: "The LORD shall repay the evildoer according to his wickedness."[2]

Broad or Narrow Road?

According to a Pew survey of over 35,000 Americans, 74 percent believe in an afterlife.[3] In another study, which asked, "Whom do you think is most likely to get into heaven?" Mother Teresa got 79 percent, Oprah 66 percent, and O. J. Simpson 19 percent. But who topped the list with 87 percent? The person responding.[4]

But when you look at the evil in the world—evil not only overseas but also in our own country—one has to wonder. Unfortunately, these surveys that conclude that the vast majority of us are going to heaven may be optimistic. I certainly don't have the final answer to this question—and no human being does—but the Scriptures tell us the disciples asked this very question: "Will only a few be saved?" And the reply was "The door to heaven is narrow."[5]

Elaborating, the Master said: "Enter by the narrow gate; for wide is the gate and broad is the way that leads to destruction, and there are many who go in by it. Because narrow is the gate and difficult is the way which leads to life and there are few who find it."[6] Regarding the Jewish people, the prophet Isaiah announced, "Though the number of the Israelites be like the sand by the sea, only [a] remnant will be saved."[7] Thus it appears that the number of individuals who *think* they will be "saved" (that is, going to heaven) is a lot higher than the Bible contends.

Many Prominent Religious Leaders Won't Be in Heaven

The scribes and Pharisees, the Jewish religious leaders of the day, were, for the most part, soundly condemned by Jesus for their self-aggrandizing: putting themselves, their reputations, and their religiosity before the common person. Some would have a horn blown so that they would be duly noticed when they gave money to the poor. The *bruised or bleeding Pharisees* meticulously avoided looking at a woman lustfully; therefore they only looked at the ground. As a result they often injured themselves as they bumped into things. Logically, the more bruised and bleeding they were, the more righteous they were. Then there was the *hump-backed Pharisee*: "Such men walked in such ostentatious humility that they were bent [over] like a hunch-back. They were so humble that they would not even lift their feet from the ground and so tripped over every obstruction they met. Their humility was self-advertising ostentation."[8]

The entire twelfth chapter of Matthew deals with this behavior and condemns the religious leaders by stating that God desires love and mercy and not self-aggrandizing religious activity. In fact, nonreligious atheists who then trusted in God would be in heaven before these self-righteous leaders. The men of the wicked city Nineveh and a pagan queen would rise up and judge those of biological Jewish heritage. Those who rely on their ancestry are going to be very surprised, as it says, "do not begin to say to yourselves, 'We have Abraham as our father.' For I say to you that God is able to raise up children to Abraham from these stones."[9]

Pharisees in All Religions

Webster's defines *Pharisee* in part as "practicing or advocating strict observance of external forms and ceremonies or religion or conduct without regard to the spirit; self-righteous; sanctimonious; hypocritical."[10] Sure, many of the scribes and Pharisees had reached the pinnacle of hypocrisy; they were the showcases of religious piety on the outside but rotten on the inside.[11] Sometimes I think the Pharisees got a bad rap; that is, they were picked out as hypocrites—when there are self-righteous religious people of virtually all religions to whom similar condemning words could rightfully be said, whether to the lowly toilet cleaner in the church or to the one responsible for the care of a large congregation, regardless of religious persuasion.

We can read of the barbaric treatment that individuals have inflicted on others in the name of religion and of the scandals up to the present time—they are certainly comparable to or worse than anything the Pharisees did. Some popes ordered inquisitions and burning at the stake of righteous Christians who differed theologically on relatively minor points of doctrine. Galileo spent the end of his life under house arrest for stating that the sun was the center of the universe. A number of religious leaders in Rwanda were allegedly key promoters of the genocide in 1994, encouraging the Tutsis to go into their churches, telling them they would be safe there, knowing that they would thus be gathered in one place to be bludgeoned to death or torched. Will they be in heaven? I seriously question that. I suspect that if Christ were strolling nearby he would have chastised them as strongly as he did the scribes and Pharisees.[12]

I am told that Muslims are considered more righteous when they have a reddish bruise on their foreheads that shows they have dutifully prayed by firmly placing their foreheads on their prayer mats. Some, to impress others, sandpaper their foreheads to make sure no one misses how spiritual they are. We Protestants have our own ways of appearing more spiritual than we actually are. I have subtly let people know how many Bible verses I have memorized or that I got up early for a "quiet time." When I pray out loud before others I am typically more concerned about how my petition sounds to the people in the room than the God of the universe. Some Protestants rely on their ancestry—born a Lutheran or an Episcopalian. So, if we are honest, all our religions have their Pharisees, and each one of us has our own self-aggrandizing tendencies. Even Christ's disciples fought over who was going to be the greatest in the kingdom of heaven.

The Irreligious Can't Be Smug

When a prominent religious figure misuses funds or falls into sexual scandal—TV has a hey-day—many have a sort of a smug, self-righteous grin, especially the irreligious. There's an attitude of "See, I told you so; you aren't so righteous after all." And yes, it is tragic when those who are supposed to be our role models fall. But lest the irreligious gloat over this, it appears to me that there are pharisaical atheists and agnostics who won't fare any better than the self-righteous religious person.

Lostness Is No Respecter of Persons

Timothy Keller, in his excellent book *The Prodigal God*, describes two groups of people as represented in the parable commonly known as "The Prodigal Son." There is the elder, self-righteous, religious brother and the younger, free-spirited son. Both men are very lost—that is, they are not bound for heaven. The elder brother says: "The good people (like us) are *in* and the bad people, who are the real problem in the world, are *out*." Whereas the younger brother says: "No, the open-minded and tolerant people are '*in*' and the bigoted, narrow-minded people, who are the real problem in the world, are '*out*'."[13] Keller comments about the elder brother:

> There are many people today who have abandoned any kind of religious faith because they see clearly that the major religions are simply full of [self-righteous] elder brothers. They have come to the conclusion that religion is one of the greatest sources of misery and strife in the world. And guess what? Jesus says . . . they are right. The anger and superiority of elder brothers, all growing out of insecurity, fear, and inner emptiness, can create a huge body of guilt-ridden, fear-ridden, spiritually blind people, which is one of the great sources of social injustice, war and violence.[14]

The overall context suggests that only one of these two sons becomes reconciled with his Father; the other one rejects the Father's love. And guess what: the one you think (and he thought) was going to heaven didn't make it—and the other did.

Thus, the evidence suggests that there are going to be a lot of unexpected people in heaven. Likewise, many in eternity will be "wailing and gnashing their teeth": countless anonymous people, self-righteous religious leaders of all stripes, as well as the infamous Hitlers.

Chapter 4

God Doesn't Always Get Everything He Wants

I am fully aware that the title of this chapter is an anathema to many readers of this book and seems counterintuitive—so I need to explain. Most of this book was written before Rob Bell's *Love Wins: A Book about Heaven, Hell, and the Fate of Every Person Who Ever Lived* was published. I believe his motivation for writing his book was much the same as mine—the seeming unfairness of the idea that individuals who have never heard of Christ will be damned to an eternity in hell, never having heard how they might go to heaven, and that individuals like Mahatma Gandhi will receive the same consequences as Hitler—an eternity in flames. Though we share a similar motivation, our conclusions are very different.[1]

In my opinion, *Love Wins* comes about as close to universalism—the belief that everyone will ultimately be saved—as one can without frankly endorsing that position. One of the tactics the gifted speaker and author uses is to raise centuries old, troubling questions, and then *imply* the answers.

For example, it seems perfectly logical that God will get what he wants. *Love Wins* says:

> God is mighty, powerful, and "in control" and [yet] billions of people will spend forever apart from this God, who is their creator, even though it's written in the Bible that "God wants all people to be saved and to come to a knowledge of the truth" (1 Tim 2). . . So does God get what God wants? . . . . Will all people be saved, or will God not get what God wants? . . . Does this magnificent, mighty, marvelous God *fail* in the end?[2]

It certainly seems logical that God can do anything; always gets whatever he wants; and certainly, will not fail in the end. Philosophers and theologians have held this position for millennia. In fact, doesn't the Bible say God can do anything?

The Lord rhetorically said to Abraham: "Is anything too hard for the LORD?"[3] Similarly, Jeremiah prayed to God saying, "There is nothing too hard for You," and God responded with "Behold, I am the LORD, the God of all flesh, Is there anything too hard for Me?"[4] But we must be careful here because these refer to God's decision and promise to grant a menopausal woman to have a child and to God's allowing Israel's enemies to take over Israel because of disobedience. In no instance was it contrary to his very character or involving two mutually exclusive choices. It is my opinion that God cannot and will not violate his very character or mutually exclusively choices.

What Rob Bell neglects, in my opinion, is that God is not only a loving God who wants all to be saved, but he is also a just and righteous God that has proclaimed the consequences for those who reject him. Both attributes must be satisfied.

Let me try and explain by taking the age-old example of "can God make a rock so heavy he can't lift it?" The answer is *he can't,* because we are defining this in such as way that the options are mutually exclusive. The nature of reality excludes both options. So God can't make a rock so heavy that he can't lift it. An easier example to comprehend is whether or not God can make a four-sided triangle. God can make a four-sided square or a three-sided triangle, but he can't make a four-sided triangle because by definition a triangle has only three sides. In fact, the Scriptures teach that there are a number of things that God can't do—such as lying.[5] Lying is contrary to his very righteous nature.

In a similar manner I believe God had a choice when he made human beings. He could make them to always do what he wanted: to obey him and never to sin. But then we would all be robots and not humans. Love must include choice. One cannot give a person the right and ability to truly love unless that person is also given the right and ability not to love—which includes the ability to hate. One cannot have the *option* to obey without the option to disobey. If God made us robots we would always do what he wanted, but we would not have free choice or be able to freely love God. A robot, by definition, is programmed to do what its maker determines.

I believe that when God made humankind he wanted individuals to have the freedom to love and worship him—and love demands the ability to choose. Giving people choice excludes the possibility of totally controlling their actions. God respects our freedom to choose. As a result, individuals can opt to obey or to disobey God—but there are consequences for one's behavior. God wants the entire world to be saved, but God's very nature—including his holiness and justice—means that people who persist in sin and reject Christ's provision will not be saved. This deeply grieves the heart of God. The scene when Christ wept over Jerusalem vividly portrays God's feelings: "O Jerusalem, Jerusalem, the one who kills the prophets and stones those who are sent to her! How often I wanted to gather your children together, as a hen gathers her brood under her wings, but you were not willing!"[6] His desire was that all Israel would be saved, but he knew their hearts. He knew that most of them would choose their own way instead of God's way.

Thus, I believe God does not get everything he wants— when two choices are mutually exclusively even God must choose which he desires the most. So if he chooses to give humans free will and the ability to love and hate—his greater desire—then it necessitates the possibility that individuals will reject him and suffer the consequences. I realize that this argument that God doesn't always get everything he wants goes against long-held views of philosophers and theologians. But I believe it is a reasonable conclusion if one reads the Bible without a preconceived grid over it.

Thus, God wanted a love relationship with humankind that necessitated choice; but his justice requires consequences for the wrong choice. We know God loves, but we also know he hates; there is a time and place where one characteristic is more apparent or trumps the other.[7] Furthermore, God is not only a loving and compassionate God, but also a just and righteous God, and at some point these qualities intersect. If you carefully read the Scriptures from cover to cover you will find hundreds of examples of his love and mercy, but likewise you see hundreds of examples of his righteous indignation and judgment. Both are attributes on a continuum and are characteristics of God. In order to satisfy both attributes he sent his son to pay the price to redeem those who are willing to accept his provision. The ultimate consequence of that decision is heaven or hell.

If you focus only on passages in the Scriptures that show God's love and mercy and have a bent in that direction you will become a universalist. On the other hand, if you focus on God's wrath and judgment you will see only sinners in the hands of an angry God. Neither extreme accurately portrays the God of the universe. God graciously provided a loving provision to satisfy his justice—the sacrifice of Jesus Christ for you and me.

Yes, as Rob Bell rightfully points out, God desires that the entire human population would go to heaven. The Scriptures clearly state: "God . . . desires all men to be saved and come to the knowledge of truth."[8] But God's righteousness and justice requires repentance and the individual's choice, saying: "He who believes in the Son has everlasting life: and he who does not believe the Son shall not see life, but the wrath of God abides on him."[9]

Now let's turn our attention to the consequences of the choice we make—the nature of heaven and hell.

Chapter 5

What Happens after Death?

A haunting question in the back of everyone's mind is what happens after death? When you think about it, there are really only four possible options: (1) We will continue in a phenomenally better state (heaven). (2) Existence will become a nightmarish experience (hell). (3) We will cease to exist. Or (4) we will be given a second chance, or some combination of these options, such as some kind of purgatory or reincarnation or shadowy afterlife. Regardless, Proverbs sums it up fairly succinctly: "For surely there is a hereafter."[1]

Furthermore, we all have a sense that there must be a purpose for existing; there must be more to life than just to have it end after seventy to possibly one hundred years in a musty, maggot-infested coffin or ashes. Even the atheist and existentialist believes human beings are unique among animals in their need to create meaning for their lives. Individuals often want to leave a legacy when they die—whether through their children or significant accomplishments. Thus we grasp at making meaning out of our earthly existence. But that desire for meaning is only truly fulfilled by discovering God's purposes for our lives.

Pascal said, "There is a God-shaped vacuum in the heart of every man which can only be filled by God."[2] Augustine added: "Thou hast made us for thyself and our hearts are restless until they find rest in thee."[3] No wonder 92 percent of Americans believe in God[4] and 74 percent believe in life after death. In fact, "polls show that eternity is not dead in the West."[5]

General Revelation

Wherever you look you see the handiwork of God's creation, whether the sun and the stars we can see or marvelous galaxies viewed through the largest telescopes or images beamed back from manned or unmanned spacecraft. The psalmist wrote: "The heavens declare the glory of God; the skies proclaim the work of his hands."[6]

On the other extreme, minute creatures make us marvel: insects that are barely visible to the naked eye yet are able to eat, digest food, defend themselves, and reproduce their kind, to say nothing about the wonders seen under the most powerful electron microscope. Then there are infinitesimal strands of DNA that produce our magnificent bodies and every living thing. And if that weren't enough, God has placed within all of us a sense, if we listen, that there must be a God. King Solomon expressed it well, saying: "He has put eternity in their hearts."[7] Theologians call this evidence of God's existence that is available to all people everywhere throughout history "general revelation."

All Responsible

The Scriptures indicate that individuals around the world throughout all time who do not have the written expression of God's Word still have, in fact, God's truths confirmed in their hearts, reinforced by the marvels of nature. Thus, people have an inherent awareness of God and the appropriate need for righteousness. In the words of the New Testament:

> [God] did not leave Himself without witness . . . because that which is known about God is evident within them; for God made it evident to them. For since the creation of the world His invisible attributes, His eternal power and divine nature, have been clearly seen, being understood through what has been made, so that they are without excuse.[8]

Don Richardson's book *Eternity in their Hearts* tells how he has studied cultures throughout the world and found within hundreds of them startling evidence of belief in the one true God. . . . [He] gives fascinating real-life examples of ways people have exhibited in their histories terms and concepts that have prepared them for the gospel. [For example] Pachacuti, the Inca king who founded Machu Picchu, the majestic fortress in Peru, accomplished something far more significant than merely building a fortress, temples or monuments. He sought, reached out and found a God far greater than any popular "god" of his own culture. And there have been others throughout the world, like him, who lived to receive the blessing of the gospel.[9]

Richardson describes how all cultures throughout the world have a belief in one true God. He says that all people groups with ancient traditions have stories that depict events similar to ones in the Old and New Testaments.[10] Such accounts resonate in our hearts and support the biblical claim that God is behind all that we experience.

Baylor University Professor Rodney Stark says, in *Discovering God*, "Religion is a universal feature of human cultures . . . from earliest times humans have been awed by the grandeur of nature. Primitive peoples clearly had a belief in a Supreme Creator, a Higher God." He goes on to say: "The many similarities of religions around the world are not evidence that they all are human inventions, but reflect a 'universal revelation' dating from the earliest times."[11]

Thus, none of us will have an alibi. The Scriptures make it clear that God has revealed enough about himself and about right and wrong to make us accountable for our response to him. The apostle Paul elaborates:

> When outsiders who have never heard of God's law follow it more or less by instinct, they confirm its truth by their obedience. They show that God's law is not something alien, imposed on us from without, but woven into the very fabric of our creation. There is something deep within them that echoes God's yes and no, right and wrong. Their response to God's yes and no will become public knowledge on the day God makes his final decision about every man and woman. The Message from God that I proclaim through Jesus Christ takes into account all these differences.[12]

The Initial Verdict

So what happens after death? The Scriptures indicate that after death each of us faces judgment by God. The Bible says, "man is destined to die once, and after that to face judgment."[13] "Each one of us will give an account of himself to God" both "the just and the unjust."[14] Randy Alcorn appropriately calls this "the judgment of faith." He elaborates, "[t]his first judgment is not to be confused with the final judgment, or what is called the judgment of works."[15] As a result of this initial judgment each of us will either face eternity in or out of God's presence.[16]

Those who have a deep faith/trust in, a commitment to God, a faith that transforms their lives, will go to heaven;[17] they will be raised to the "resurrection of life."[18] The true God-follower will put on immortality. The Scriptures declare: "For our earthly bodies, the ones we have now that can die, must be transformed into heavenly bodies that cannot perish but will live forever."[19] All true followers of God will live forever in God's wonderful presence.

Eternal Splendor—Heaven

All who have responded to God's gracious gift of eternal life will enjoy heaven forever. But the notion that we will be floating on clouds, playing harps, and singing endlessly in a church choir is a fairytale and not supported by God's word.

The images used in the Bible to depict heaven are of the most ideal place one could imagine, which God has prepared for those who love him.[20] In fact, we cannot imagine the wonders of heaven to be enjoyed by all of our five senses.

It will be a place where we will have resurrected, eternal bodies that are without pain, illness, or decline. We will be able to retain the pleasant memories of this life, enjoy and develop new relationships with others, and will have the ability to pursue new and rewarding activities forever in God's grand cosmos.

I believe it is real, and when my time on earth is up, I actually look forward to what is ahead. I will not take the time or space to describe it in further detail here, but refer you to some of the excellent material available.[21]

Rewards in Heaven

Some evangelical/fundamental Christians convey the idea that if you pray the "sinner's prayer" (confessing your sins and asking Christ into your heart) you will go to heaven and experience *equal* blessings with everyone else there. Like an off-on switch—it's either all or nothing. If this is what the Scriptures taught, I would hold to it even if it intuitively seems unfair; but I don't think that is what the Scriptures teach. Since the Reformation Protestants have had such an aversion to anything that might be interpreted as good "works" that we have, in my opinion, often distorted the Scriptures. We will have more to say about this in a later chapter.

The Scriptures teach that how we have lived out our *life of faith* makes a difference in heaven. Many passages in the Scriptures indicate there will be different rewards given in heaven, depending on how one has lived his or her life of faith here on earth. For example, it says some will be saved "as by fire," some will rule over a few cities, while others rule over many cities. There will even be those who sit at God's right hand.[22]

Robert Ervin Hough says in *The Christian after Death:* "While the salvation will, therefore, be the same for all the redeemed, the glory of each will not be the same, the difference being determined by the fruits of their lives on earth."[23] Randy Alcorn adds: "The doctrine of eternal rewards hinges on specific acts of faithfulness done on Earth . . . and are brought into Heaven with us."[24] John Piper supports this understanding, saying: "Both Jesus and Paul teach that believers will receive differing rewards in accord with the degree that their faith expresses itself in acts of service and love and righteousness."[25]

The Alternative—Eternal Separation from God

Sadly, as a result of each person's response to God's gracious offer of heaven, those who refuse or are just unresponsive to God's gift of salvation will face eternal separation from God and the splendor that he desires to give every person in the world. This eternal separation, otherwise known as hell, will be permanent.

The Traditional View of Hell

There are a number of verses in the Bible that describe hell as a boiling caldron of brimstone where "the worm does not die." The literal or traditional view of hell is unending conscious torment in a *literal pit of lava*. This view was established and fairly well sealed by Augustine and the Catholic Church in the middle of the first millennium and continues to the present day.

There are some very strong verses that seem to endorse this view,[26] and a large segment of Christianity adamantly sanctions it. I remember hearing a sermon about hell with illustrations at nine years of age—and it was terrifying. Though most evangelicals/fundamentalists hold to this view, they often seem very uncomfortable elaborating in any detail on what they actually mean.

It seems to me that many who hold to this position are concerned that letting any "unsaved" person off the hook from smoldering endlessly in a bottomless pit of literal brimstone will take away the incentive for individuals to accept God's gracious gift of everlasting life in heaven and reduce the urgency for missions. The height of threatening people with eternal torment came in the Middle Ages when the Church used these tactics to control people and generate money through indulgences. Such an extreme message may well have worked then, but to most people today it seems preposterous and, I believe, is an added reason why Western society is basically turned off by religion.

If I believed this is what God teaches I would hold to it—but I don't believe it is what the Bible teaches. It seems to me that holding to hell being an endless caldron of writhing in equal agony for *every* nonbeliever is actually counterproductive, often causing the person outside the church to dismiss the whole idea of future accountability and its consequences as ludicrous. It makes God into an unjust god who would be equivalent to a judge in our society doling out only two penalties for all crimes: setting them free or giving them the death sentence. It causes so many college students, even from good evangelical churches, to dismiss out of hand all the claims of Scripture. Furthermore, I believe it is the reason universalism is as popular as it is.

Metaphorical View of Hell

Many others endorse a literal, conscious, tormenting hell but view these descriptions as metaphors.[27] I place myself in this camp, believing that the biblical description of eternal brimstone and fire where the worm is unable to die is the most vivid description of a place where one would not want to be. It is a *literal place* of *painful physical and conscious suffering.* I believe Billy Graham is of this persuasion. I remember him saying he wondered if hell was the absence of God and one spinning endlessly into outer space. He has been quoted as saying: "The only thing I could say for sure is that hell means separation from God. . . . That is going to be hell. When it comes to a literal fire, I don't preach it because I'm not sure about it."[28]

Origin of Hell

Let's digress for a moment and think about the origin of evil. Lucifer, also known as Satan, was the most esteemed angel in heaven, who started a revolution to resist God's will. He rallied a number of angelic followers in his resistance. God threw them all out of his presence, and ever since they have been trying to get back at God through you and me. They are the prime instigators leading men and women down through the ages into evil and rebellion against God and each other. If you stop for a moment and think of all the misery they have caused throughout time, hell makes a lot of sense. Thus, hell was primarily made for Satan and his angelic disciples who will ultimately face severe, conscious, eternal punishment [29] I suspect somewhere behind Satan and his angelic followers will be the Hitler types, mobsters, serial rapists, and the like. Following them, other human beings will also experience conscious retribution, first for resisting God's gracious overtures to them and secondarily for how they have lived out their sinful lives.

Differing Consequences in Hell

Often traditional evangelicals/fundamentalists convey the idea that all who do not "accept Christ" will experience the same horrible, never-ending, unimaginable suffering—whether one is Satan, Hitler, or the average person who has rejected God's gift of salvation. And again, it's like an on-off switch: you either go to heaven or hell—equal bliss on one hand, or equally horrible suffering on the other hand. If the Scriptures taught this, I would hold to it; but, in fact, I don't believe this is what God's Word declares.

Just as there will be degrees of rewards in heaven, there clearly will be varying degrees of punishment in hell— depending on the knowledge the individual has and how one has lived out his or her life of rejecting God. Erwin Lutzer, theologian and senior pastor of Moody Church in Chicago, says, "There are degrees of punishment in hell and degrees of reward in heaven."[30] Likewise, William Crockett says, "Hell is a dreadful place, but not a place of equal suffering. Some will receive lesser punishment, some more"[31]

Don't get me wrong—hell will be hell for everyone who is there. It will not be a high school class reunion at a local bar reminiscing about the pranks one got away with on earth. It will be far closer to a trial for capital punishment in which God will be the judge and jury and will have total access to the hard drives of all of our thoughts, motives, and actions, including things that we may have forgotten.[32] Those who have not reconciled with God prior to dying will stand speechless and defenseless. After that initial condemnation, there will be the sentencing process where lesser or greater degrees of punishment will be doled out. In part, this will be dependent on how much a person knew of God's truths and remained unresponsive, but also, in fact, on the degree of evil the person has actually committed.[33]

Two Possibilities

The Bible is exceedingly clear that hell is real and that there will be differing degrees of punishment in hell.[34] Erwin Lutzer says: "hell will not be the same for everyone."[35] However, it is not at all clear as to *how* God will achieve this—thus one is almost forced to speculate on the exact nature of hell.[36] It seems reasonable to consider two possible options. First, that hell will go on endlessly for everyone who is not "saved," but that there will be differing intensities of suffering in hell. Theologian Edward Fudge says, "The actual process of destruction [referring to hell] may well involve conscious pain that differs in magnitude in each individual case—Scripture seems to indicate that it will."[37]

The second possibility is that *at some point* in "eternity" a lesser penalty for some might be annihilation. Note I say: "at some point in eternity." *I do not believe that hell and annihilation are synonymous.* For example, there are verses that say, "do not be afraid of those who kill the body, and after that have no more that they can do. But . . . Fear Him who, after He has killed, has power to cast into hell."[38] This clearly indicates hell is worse than death. Furthermore, there are verses in the Bible that suggest eternal conscious/physical torment[39] and others that suggest individuals at some point will cease to exist.[40] Robert A. Peterson, professor of theology and a traditionalist, says, "Much of the New Testament vocabulary of destruction could be understood as teaching either traditionalism (eternal conscious suffering) or annihilationism."[41]

The idea that *all* human beings are immortal started with early philosophers like Plato, who influenced the church fathers in the first five to six hundred years AD, and this concept of the immortality of the soul remains embedded in most of Christianity today. Edward Fudge elaborates that "Plato taught that each person also has a soul that is immortal and cannot die." He goes on to explain:

> Soon after the time of the apostolic fathers, certain converts from Greek philosophy, known as the apologists, brought into the church the pagan doctrine of the immortality of the soul. . . . Plato . . . declares, "Every soul is immortal". . . in this way the stones of pagan Greek philosophy began to pave the road to today's traditionalism.[42]

It is absolutely clear that individuals in heaven are immortal. However, the idea of immortality in hell depends on how one interprets some verses in the Bible regarding the nature of hell. The highly respected theologian and Anglican leader John Stott has stated: "the ultimate annihilation of the wicked should at least be accepted as a legitimate, biblically founded alternative to their eternal conscious torment."[43] Roger E. Olson, professor of theology at Baylor University, says,

The rise of interest in and affirmation of annihilationism has predictably given rise to a reaction; many conservative evangelical theologians have resurrected the old polemical labels of heresy and aberrational teaching to marginalize those evangelicals who would dare to embrace a belief that was once relegated to the sectarian margins of Protestantism. This hardly seems like a valuable expenditure of time and energy. Annihilationism does not strike at the heart of the gospel or even deny any major Christian belief; it is simply a reinterpretation of hell. More importantly, its harsh condemnation by a few fundamentalists should not deter Christians from accepting one another as equally believers in the gospel of Jesus Christ in spite of differences of opinion about the nature of hell. Contrary to what some fundamentalist critics have charged, annihilationism is not tantamount to universalism. . . . It is simply a minority view of the nature of hell, not a denial of hell.[44]

Earlier this year I had a skiing accident and fractured my ankle. Subsequent to that my sodium dropped to a level "marginal with life"—my internist told me later. I felt an indescribably awful feeling, that, though I am a physician, I found difficult to describe. I couldn't remember my own telephone number. I went to the emergency room, and the diagnosis was totally missed and I was sent home. For over a week, I thought, "I really don't want to kill myself—I don't really want to die; but I certainly don't want to live this way." I remember thinking many times, "I wonder if this is something of what hell feels like? Annihilation would be better than an ongoing existence like this." Every waking hour was hell. I didn't know where to turn—what to do—I wasn't thinking clearly enough to make rational decisions or to press my case. If I could have jumped out of my skin I would have. The only respite I got was a few hours of oblivion after taking a sleeping pill at night. I dreaded the next day. What I can tell you for sure is that *if* I had only the options of endless discomfort like that or annihilation, I would unquestionably pick the latter.

Which of these two options most closely resembles what hell will be like—I can't be sure. What I do want to be sure of is that, either way, I'm not going there. I believe that we can have that assurance.

Purgatory or a Second Chance—Don't Count On It

Some theologians and entire religious groups hold that after death some individuals will be able to get right with God in purgatory—a sort of cleansing to get ready for heaven. I see no basis in the Bible for this idea.[45] Others suggest an outright second chance. This is one way to solve the seemingly unjust prospect of God's condemning those who have, allegedly, never been given the opportunity to hear and respond to God's good news. Admittedly there are five brief passages in the Bible that are difficult to explain and may possibly present this view.[46] I can't be dogmatic that God won't do something like that, especially for those who have had no opportunity to hear about God's redemptive plan. However, the preponderance of Scripture comes down on the side that urges one to make a decision while one can in this life, and not to count on a second chance.

Passages such as "Choose you this day whom you will serve" and "As it is appointed unto man once to die and after that the judgment" indicate the time to make a decision is now. Furthermore, in one clear example, the selfish rich man who went to hell, shunning the needs of the poor, had absolutely no second chance though he obviously wanted one.[47] In fact, in eternity those crying out for a second chance will be told: "Depart from Me, all you workers of iniquity."[48] To place any confidence in such an idea is about as wise as getting on an airplane with known faulty engines and hoping you make it to your destination. Forget about a second chance. The Bible says: "now is the accepted time; behold, now is the day of salvation."[49]

Conclusion

The Scriptures teach that *what we believe* and *how we live out* our lives will affect our eternal future. The wonderful news is that God wants to give us a glorious, never-ending life in heaven with resurrected physical bodies far exceeding anything we can imagine.

Chapter 6

God Can Work through Many Religions

A recent cover story in *Christianity Today* reported the finding of a national survey conducted by the Pew Forum on Religion and Public Life stating that fifty-two percent of all *Christians* in America believe that non-Christian faiths can lead to eternal life. Furthermore, it said, "More people than ever doubt that anyone has a corner on truth."[1]

Do I agree with that? Well, yes and no. First off—I don't think any religion on the face of the earth today has a corner on God's truth nor has *all the truth*. My guess is that current *formalized* religions vary from having some to having a lot of God's truth—but when all is said and done none even begin to approach 100 percent.

As I indicated in chapter 1, all organized religions and denominations that hold the Bible to be authoritative, add or subtract from the Scriptures. In order to have a "religion," it is incumbent to codify it, and once a person or group does that, they interpret what they think God is saying in order to have a cohesive system of theology. None of us humans or institutions gets this all correct. I believe God tolerates a certain amount of our error, especially if it is made in "ignorance."[2] That does not alter the fact that God will hold us accountable to him for what we do know and teach and how we live.

Judaism certainly had a lot of baggage at the beginning of the first millennium. Even the early Christian church struggled with this—how much of the Jewish laws should the non-Jewish believer be required to observe to be saved?[3] What is baggage and what is essential?

Though God can work through many religions to bring us to himself, in fact some religions can make it more difficult to comprehend God's truth.

The closer one sticks to the Scriptures the greater the likelihood of retaining the truth. However, once one starts to explain the Scriptures, develop a systematized theology, or attempt to elucidate the many inevitable issues on which the Scriptures are more silent, assumptions have to be made and the likelihood of error greatly increases. The Scriptures tell us God's ways are higher than our ways and his thoughts higher than ours. I believe the best analogy is that the spiritual realm is three dimensional and we as human beings are only capable of seeing spiritual realities in two dimensions; we see a pyramid as a square or as a triangle. I'm not so sure God wants us to "know" every detail; but he provides the essentials and wants us to live out our lives as his word teaches. Therefore, there will always be mystery—some areas where we must accept ambiguity. All this applies not only to any organized religion but also to a book like this. I start out with a body of facts clearly aligned with the Scriptures and the likelihood of truth, hopefully, approaches 100 percent. But then there are areas that the Scriptures do not clearly explain or in some cases, are totally silent. So I am forced either to leave large gaps in explaining parts of the issues or to use suggestions from the Scriptures and build a cohesive case. We all long for clarity, but along with our efforts to clarify comes the possibility for error. *Fortunately, we don't have to get all of our doctrine exactly right to enter heaven—but we do need a heart that truly desires to know, believe, and obey God's truth to the extent revealed to us.*

A. W. Tozer speaks to this topic:

> Apart from Christ and His inspired apostles probably no believer or company of believers in the history of the world has ever held the truth in total purity. . . . No believer, however pure his heart or however obedient his life, has ever been able to receive it as it shines from the Throne unmodified by his own mental stuff. . . . The conclusion of the matter is that we should not assume that we have all the truth and that we are mistaken in nothing.[4]

In fact, all religious leaders, whether they are called popes, apostles, prophets, bishops, priests, ministers, rabbis, or imams, can get it wrong. Even the original apostle Peter, a "pillar of the church" got it wrong at times.[5] We can see in Acts 15 that even when the apostles and elders met to make decisions they struggled to come to conclusions about many of the issues.

While fulfilling my role in church leadership, I made many decisions that, at the time, I thought were right—but there are some I would make differently today if I had the opportunity. Even the apostle Paul said that if he, as one of the apostles of the early church, or an angel from heaven declared something different than what is in the Scriptures—they are wrong. This is true for all leaders and ecclesiastical bodies. For many details of the Scriptures "are past finding out!"[6] The apostle Paul at times said, "*I think . . .*" regarding certain matters he wasn't sure about.[7] The Scriptures tell us that "now we know [only] in part."[8] And in case you are wondering, yes, my religion has baggage with it—and yes, I expect that I do also. Does this book get it all "right"—I think so, I hope so—but I certainly can't be dogmatic.

Once men or women get a hold of religious truth, it will become contaminated—some religions a lot more than others. But God, almost in spite of many religions, reaches out to individuals, looking for those whose heart desires to respond to him.[9] Thus, it seems to me, that despite the error in many religions, God sees the heart and uses whatever is at his disposal to lead us into greater truth.

No Religion, Church, or Sacrament Is *Essential* for Heaven

Early in Catholicism Bishop Cyprian of Carthage proclaimed that "*Outside the church there is no salvation.*"[10] Later, seven sacraments were defined that could only be administered by the Church and were necessary for salvation. This was highly coercive on the Church's part. If you didn't have the blessing of the Church, you couldn't go to heaven—you were going to hell—it was that simple and clear cut. They held the keys to your eternal future. Luther put God back in the center and emphasized that God's forgiveness and grace cannot be sold and bought but was a gift of God. He rejected all but two of these sacraments and concluded that they could be administered by spiritual people outside the Roman Catholic Church; thus one could go to heaven without the blessing of the Catholic Church, but other humans were necessary to make it possible.

What is essential for salvation has been in contention since the early days of Christianity. In the very early church circumcision was considered essential, as was keeping the Old Testament laws such as avoiding pork and observing ritual washings. Only at the Jerusalem Council was it determined that circumcision was not mandatory for salvation.[11] Since then so many issues have come up to split believers. Take the issue of baptism alone: Is it essential for salvation; if so, by immersion or sprinkling, before or after one "believes," forward or backward, once or three times? And so it goes with doctrine after doctrine. No wonder there are so many different groups of people worshiping the same God. So often, I believe, we have lost the simplicity that is in Christ.[12]

Don't get me wrong, *appropriate* spiritual fellowship, encouragement, and leadership are crucial in our spiritual growth; but your and my salvation—going to heaven—is *not dependent* on any other human being, religious organization, or sacrament. The Scriptures are very clear that no human being, church, or agency is the mediator or necessary element between us and God.[13] Christopher J. H. Wright correctly says: "salvation is clearly not something you can 'get' from religion considered as a set of human activities or aspirations. The very question sometimes asked in the debate over other faiths, 'Is there salvation in other religions?' is highly misleading, since it embodies a false premise—namely, that salvation is something you get from *any* religion."[14] It has been appropriately stated that "Christ . . . is not the property of the Church but the Lord of the Church."[15] Religions tend to focus on what one does for God or to get God's favor. God's good news is just the opposite of this—the gospel is that God has come to us in Christ, embraced us, forgiven us and called us to be his children for time and eternity.

Many Religions *Can* Lead to God

The Scriptures tell us that "the Lord is not willing that any should perish, but that all should come to repentance."[16] Thus, I believe that God desires that everyone would come to a right relationship with him and spend eternity in the splendors of heaven.[17]

We have already seen how he uses general revelation—the marvels of creation—to cause us to pause and contemplate that there must be an intelligent creator behind our spectacular cosmos. We have discussed Don Richardson's documenting startling evidence of belief in one true God down through history and throughout numerous cultures.[18]

Furthermore, God has on occasion used various specific means to communicate to mankind including clouds and pillars of fire to lead people, burning bushes, soft voices, and yes, even a donkey to speak to an individual! God's Spirit continues to woo people to himself and will use sundry means to achieve his purposes. We, therefore, must be careful that we don't limit the avenues that God can use to bring individuals to himself.

Religions are another means that God uses. They're

humanity's imperfect way to seek God, to respond to God's nudging, and to worship him. Many religions have in common a sense of sin causing alienation from God, a conviction that some sort of sacrifice or atonement is necessary to bridge the gap between God and humankind, and a belief in the need for some sort of mediator.

Since religions are humanity's attempts to find God, some do a better job at this than others. However, we have to be careful that we don't have too myopic a view of how God works, even as Christ's disciples did. It is true some make the process almost impossible, even as Christ chastised the religious leaders of his day for actually making it more difficult to find and know God. Others, fortunately, facilitate our knowing the true God.

Chapter 1 showed how individuals from divergent religious backgrounds have ultimately come to a right relationship with God. Along this line I am reminded of Mary Harris, who tells of a yearning for meaning in her life and felt that she had found her answer in Buddhism, which emphasized compassion, loving-kindness, and personal transformation. Though she embraced Buddhism, she still felt an inner void and was eventually led to the life and teaching of Christ. She now says she has found true peace.[19]

All Religions Can Lead Away from God

Religions do vary in the amount of truth they contain, and obviously, the more truth, the more likely it will point to the God of all truth. Despite what I have said in other parts of this book, *I firmly believe doctrine is very important.* We should aim to get it as close to God's truth as possible but realize a lot of people will be in heaven with imperfect doctrine.

But from here it gets stickier, as all religions can have the opposite effect—yes, they can all lead away from God. A religion that has a lot of truth and very little love can lead people away from God just as much, or sometimes more, than a religion that has less of God's truth in it. Yes, a good religion lacking demonstrable love can drive people away from God and actually be a hindrance. Christ strongly criticized many of the religious leaders of his day because they knew a lot of the truth but manifested little love and thus were a significant hindrance, actually preventing others from entering God's kingdom.[20]

I think of a patient I saw many years ago as a psychiatrist. As a child he was dragged to a church that sounded like it genuinely taught the "truth." However, as seen through my patient's eyes, the church leaders were harsh, and his father would beat him with a three-inch belt with a "big brass buckle on it." Decades later, this man was struggling in my office with what to do with God—that is, the God of his father and his father's church.

Thus, religions of all kinds—or people in religions of all kinds—can hinder people from knowing God. Yet at the same time, God uses all sorts of vehicles to draw men and women to himself, including religions, and not infrequently in spite of religions. "For in Christ, neither our most conscientious religion nor disregard of religion amounts to anything. What matters is something far more interior: faith expressed in love."[21]

Chapter 7

You Can't Get to Heaven
By Good Works

During the Middle Ages, the Roman Catholic Church deemed seven sacraments necessary for salvation, and these could only be administered by the Church. Thus the Church became an essential ingredient for one to go to heaven.[1] Without the Church's blessing you were damned to hell. Later, the Church became more self-serving by selling indulgences—spiritual currency benefiting the Church's coffers. Through these indulgences an individual could decrease their time, or someone else's time, in purgatory. These certificates were sold by professional pardoners utilizing aggressive marketing practices *to buy your way out of purgatory or hell,* called by some a "get-out-of purgatory-free card."[2] It was salvation in exchange for money.

In fact, Johann Tetzel, a Dominican priest, preached on behalf of Pope Leo X in 1517:

All of you, run for the salvation of your souls. . . .

Listen now, God and St. Peter call *you,* Consider

the salvation of *your* souls and those of *your loved ones* departed. . . . Listen to the voices of *your dead* relatives and friends, beseeching *you* and saying, "Pity us, pity us. We are in dire torment from which you can redeem us for a pittance." Do *you* not wish to? Open *your* ears. Hear the father saying to his son, the mother to her daughter, "We bore you, nourished you, brought you up, left you our fortunes, and you are so cruel and hard that now you are not willing for so little to set us free. Will you let us lie here in flames?" . . . Remember *you* are able to release them, for *as soon as the coin in the coffer rings, the soul from Purgatory springs.*[3]

The Church, in my opinion, was doing exactly what the Jewish scribes and Pharisees had done previously—substituting their own conditions for God's grace. Such action is detestable to God, and if Christ was physically walking the face of the earth at the time I think he would have been as outspoken against the Church as he was with the scribes and Pharisees.

Then along came Martin Luther, a highly dedicated and sensitive Catholic priest. He sincerely wanted to be a good Catholic but was torn apart internally by guilt despite all the works of penance he could do. Furthermore, he was a little obsessive compulsive which further complicated his years of intense internal struggling. Luther reacted to the clear abuses that made a person dependent on one's own effort and the Church for one's salvation—a clear violation of Scripture. There were two particular problems with the doctrine of that time: the Church not only became necessary for salvation, it also prescribed specific works that an individual had to perform to be saved, which negated the very sacrifice that only Christ can do on our behalf. Luther couldn't live with himself if he didn't challenge this practice—even if it meant being burned at the stake; thus the birthing of Protestantism. The Protestant rallying point since then has been *sola fide*, by *faith alone*.

Reliance on Good Works—An Anathema to God

It is clear from the Scriptures that any *reliance* on good works is an anathema to God. Again, some Pharisees epitomize such an attitude. They were called the *"ever-reckoning . . . Pharisee."* Such an individual was "forever reckoning up his good deeds . . . and believed that every good deed he did put God a little further in his debt."[4] Both religious and irreligious people do this today. In the process they may actually do a lot of truly wonderful deeds—helping the downtrodden in all sorts of ways. But if any of us think we are going to get to heaven through such a means—we are dead wrong.

The Gospels include an account of a very rich young ruler coming to Christ and asking the central question of this book: "Good Teacher, *what good thing shall I do that I may have eternal life?*"[5] Christ replies with a preposterous answer to drive his point home. He tells him to sell all he had, give the proceeds to the poor, and follow him, a migrant preacher who didn't have a roof over his head or a cent in his pocket. The young man was asking how he could through following religious laws and doing good works *earn* heaven. Christ was telling him *it can't be done that way—you're on the wrong path—an impossible path—you've got it all wrong!* All our religious efforts will never be enough to save you or me and earn our way into heaven. The

Scriptures teach: "For by grace you have been saved through faith, and that not of yourselves; it is the gift of God, not of works, lest anyone should boast."[6]

Bill Gates was the richest man in the world until he started giving his money away. If he gave every last penny he has to the many wonderful philanthropic projects he and his wife, Melinda, are supporting, and ended up on the street begging for money to buy food, such good works would not get him into heaven. No wonder the disciples were flabbergasted at their teacher's response, questioning: "Who then can be saved?"[7]

The Apostle Paul elaborates further, saying, "though I bestow all my goods to feed the poor, and though I give my body to be burned . . . it profits me nothing."[8] The message is clear that by our works we can never *earn* forgiveness or salvation—whether it is by our own efforts or that of any organized religion. Going down this path is barking up the wrong tree. Religions tend to emphasis what we do for God or to earn God's merit; a true Christ-follower is overwhelmed by what God has done for him or her. The Scriptures say that all of our righteous acts, our very best deeds, will never get us into heaven. In fact, if we think we can get past the pearly gates through our noblest self-efforts, it is an utter insult to God.[9] This has been the rallying point of Protestantism ever since Luther. No one will ever get to heaven by his or her own goodness, *period*.

This part Protestantism got right, but I'm not as sure about the other half of the message!

Chapter 8

You Can't Get to Heaven
Without Good Works

The rallying point of Protestantism since the Reformation has been *sola fide, faith alone.* Truly our salvation is strictly through faith in the completed work of Christ. Clarifying this truth has unshackled many from the bondage of "works" since the 1400s. This understanding of Scripture has clarified that no church or other religious organization is necessary to be saved. A church or religion may be helpful—but it is not an essential ingredient. Likewise, all of a person's good works will not earn one's salvation. As discussed earlier, relying on such a means is an anathema to God. But this very truth has created tremendous problems for Protestants ever since the Reformation. There has been confusion as to the appropriate role of works and whether a transformed life is essential for salvation. How do good works fit in? Can you pray the sinners prayer—that's it—and go to heaven? Can you have saving faith and live like the devil? I don't think so![1]

Dwight Carlson

Protestant Reaction Formation

In psychiatry we have a term called "reaction formation." Basically it means that if a person, or group of people, strongly disapproves of a given position there is a tendency to go to the opposite extreme to counteract the position that one dislikes. We often see this in politics. It appears to me this has occurred in Protestantism relative to the issue of good works. C. S. Lewis appropriately sums up the problem:

> [The Devil] always sends errors into the world in pairs—pairs of opposites. And he always encourages us to spend a lot of time thinking which is worse. You see why, of course? He relies on your extra dislike of the one error to draw you gradually into the opposite one.[2]

Luther's reaction formation against any emphasis on works took him to the point of virtually throwing out certain books in the New Testament—especially the book of James, which he called the "epistle of straw" and questioned its even being part of the Scriptures.[3] James was probably written by the half-brother of Christ, and articulates the role of works and faith. It says, "faith by itself, if it does not have works, is dead."[4]

The Third Rail of Protestantism

The role of works in the Christian life might well be called the untouchable third rail of Protestantism, especially in the evangelical/fundamental wing of Protestantism. It is such a highly charged issue that talking about any works or change in character in the Christian life relative to salvation must be avoided at all costs. Dallas Willard alludes to this taboo in *The*

Divine Conspiracy: "To insist that something more than mere faith must be present [for salvation] would be to add 'works' on to pure grace. And that, *we know from our Protestant cultural heritage, cannot be done.*"[5]

Some have tried to deal with this issue with the concept of "cheap grace"—that is, grace that does not involve a change in behavior. If we think God's grace is cheap, we are greatly mistaken. It was not cheap for God, and it will not be cheap for us. Others have emphasized "lordship salvation"—which moves the issue in the right direction. There is reason to question if anyone will have eternal life with God if God isn't the Lord and master of his or her life.

I introduced Job in chapter 1 as a pagan who ultimately had a right relationship with God and will be in heaven. When you read the book of Job, it is clear his very life centered on God. It was not a casual relationship that he fostered a couple of hours a week on a holy day and then lived like everyone else the rest of the time. God was the very center of his life, and everything else flowed out of that relationship. Everything he had was entrusted to God. So it will be with us. If we have the eternal kind of life that will spend time without end in God's splendor, then our lives on earth will reflect that relationship with God. It will be in our very DNA; it will be the center of our lives.

As one reads through the four Gospels, for every verse that Christ speaks about the importance of faith such as "believe in me" or "your faith has made you well" there are twelve verses elaborating on how we practically should live out that faith, that is, works.[6] Examples of the latter are "go and sin no more" and "take up [your] cross and follow me."[7] Yes, our faith is crucial and we will never get to heaven without total reliance on the work of Christ for our salvation. But the preponderance of Christ's teaching emphasizes how we actually live out our life of faith. For the most part evangelicals are terrified that if one talks about good works at all it will lead down the slippery slope to working for salvation—thus they tend to overreact and in the process distort what the Scriptures really teach about the appropriate place of works.

When we are saved from the wrath of God, it makes us drastically different people—transformed—and we will produce good works in the form of good fruit. Our lives will manifest the very nature of God.[8]

A Principle throughout All Time

As we elaborated on in chapter 1, those who were saved before Christ physically walked on planet earth had a saving faith that transformed their lives. They manifested that faith in a life consistent with being a follower of God. Hebrews 11 is often referred to as the "Hall of Faith," reciting in great detail the stalwarts in the Old Testament and their faith. As you read it carefully, it's more about the *evidence* of faith in the lives of various Old Testament saints. It is a resume of Old Testament believers who sought and pleased God, were willing to sacrifice, refused evil identification, were willing to suffer, including martyrdom—all works exemplifying their faith. *It is a story of manifestations of faith in the lives of godly men and women.* Moreover, it moves to a great crescendo in the first three verses of chapter 12, telling us to lay aside not only sin but also unnecessary impediments and run with endurance the race that is set before us, following the example of the One who was willing to sacrifice his very life in obedience to God.

That is our example of faith lived out in one's life. Moreover, the need to act in accordance with one's faith runs from the beginning of the Old Testament down through every major Christian tradition in all of church history.[9]

The Good Tree

If our faith is not evidenced by a radically changed life, something is dreadfully wrong. In fact, the Scriptures say that in Christ one becomes a thoroughly new person.[10] We are transformed. *One is never saved by the good works, but faith that saves will always produce good works.*[11]

The best analogy of this truth is the one Christ actually used: that a good tree cannot produce bad fruit—that we will be known for what we are by our fruit.[12] An orange tree produces oranges because the DNA in its seed and every cell is that of an orange tree. If the seed has good soil, moisture, and sunlight, it will produce oranges. It cannot, not, produce oranges. If we have the DNA of a believer in Christ we will produce good fruit. Jesus says: "Not everyone who says to Me, Lord, Lord, shall enter the kingdom of heaven, but he who does the will of My Father in heaven."[13] Another passage says that "whoever does not practice righteousness is not of God."[14]

In all fairness to Martin Luther, he had a more balanced view of faith and works than is often appreciated. He wrote:

> Faith cannot help doing good works constantly. It doesn't stop to ask if good works ought to be done, but before anyone asks, it already has done them and continues to do them without ceasing. *Anyone who does not do good works in this manner is an unbeliever.*[15]

I sometimes wonder if Luther were alive today and could see how blasé many Protestants are on the appropriate place of good works, would he come down hard on the necessity of good fruit in the Christian's life?

In Conclusion

All of our good works can never, ever get us into heaven; our best deeds are but scum—all our personal righteousness is like filthy rags to God in terms of solving our sin problem and reconciling us to God. On the other hand, a saving relationship with God inevitably transforms our lives so they will produce good fruit.

Some have raised the question about the thief on the cross going to heaven without apparent "good works." I would respond by saying that his publicly asking Christ to remember him in Paradise was a "good work"; furthermore, like any "deathbed conversion," I believe that God knows the individual's heart and that if the person had the opportunity to live, he or she would manifest good works. It would be in their DNA from the moment of their new birth in Christ.

If our lives do not look Christ-like, if they don't look drastically different from those of the world around us, then one needs to question the genuineness of one's faith and whether one is bound for heaven.

Therefore, you can't get to heaven without a life transformed by God, and such a life will manifest good works. As Christ said, "every good tree bears good fruit. A good tree cannot bear bad fruit, nor can a bad tree bear good fruit. . . . Therefore by their fruits you will know them."[16]

Chapter 9

Christians Should Stop Westernizing the World

A brilliant physician friend of mine alleges that "religions are the blight of mankind." He contends that they have been the cause of untold suffering and most of the wars that have plagued the world. He blames our current East-West conflict on Christianity, Judaism, and Islam. He was raised in the church and for the most part has thrown it all overboard, contending that the curse of mankind is religious people of all stripes, especially all fundamentalists. His solution is to do away with all religions, thus making the world a much happier and safer place to live—or so he contends.

Institutionalized Christianity *Can Be* Destructive

In part I have to agree with my friend. Though religions have done a lot of good—which we will talk about later—they have also caused much suffering. *In fact, one of the greatest disservices that Christians have done has been to try to "Westernize" or some would say "Christianize" the world.* This process started not long after Christianity became the official religion of the Roman Empire. We see it most notably with the Crusades: a toxic mixture of religious zeal and political force joined to "take back" the Holy Land, allegedly for Christ. These zealots rode into battle with crosses on their shields and swords in their hands to restore the principles of Christ who, incidentally, told Peter to put down his sword. The irony here is that Jesus himself refused to defend himself even when his very life was at stake.

Not long after, the Church, backed by the political powers of the day, in its fanaticism to eradicate heresy, undertook the inquisitions. They sought to stamp out by burning alive—not the murderer, the swindler, or even the adulterer—but the highly conscientious believer who differed in minor ways from the religious establishment. Add to this the colonization of the Americas, Africa, and parts of Asia, in which Christian Europe used force, often enhanced by Christianity, to extract the wealth of non-Western nations.

In the late 1800s it was debated whether it was the "white man's burden" to impart their culture to non-whites, a concept often used as a justification for colonialism.[1] Largely as a result of Christian support, slavery survived into the nineteenth century. The Christian church, for the most part, looked the other way while Hitler's incinerators cremated the Jews.[2] Even more recently the Ku Klux Klan with "Christian" elements lynched blacks,[3] while Catholics and Protestants killed each other in Ireland.

Those of us in the West believe in and are committed to democracy. Frankly, I believe that if the people of a given region are sufficiently mature, democracy is, hands down, the best form of government. However, when Westerners claim to be bringing democracy we so often impose our own agendas and culture. Moreover, much of the world equates "Western" with "Christian." They see the influence of any Westerners—whether to introduce democracy, increase business revenues, or evangelize—as westernizing the world with all of its baggage of sexually explicit movies, drunkenness, and moral decay. Often the church's well-intended efforts are seen as "Christianizing" them, meaning imposing Western culture and religion on them.

A good example of how Christianizing and Westernizing get intermingled in the Eastern mind is one told by Mazhar Mallouhi, whom I discussed in chapter 2. On one of his first visits to the United States as a new follower of Jesus, he saw a car with a big bumper sticker saying "Jesus is Lord" filled with girls in skimpy bikinis. No wonder the East gets Christianity and Westernization mixed up—and we don't help matters.[4]

Mazhar Mallouhi had a deep interest in spiritual things at the early age of six and began attending Qur'anic school, but soon his feelings turned negative towards Islam. His spiritual hunger drove him to philosophy and Eastern religions, which didn't satisfy either. His impression of Christianity was that it was a tool of colonial oppression—an extension of the Crusades continuing to the present in the Middle East. In fact, in most of the Muslim world, calling oneself a Christian does not mean what it does to Western evangelicals. For evangelicals, it has a spiritual meaning: one has experienced new birth in Christ and follows him as Lord. "In most of the Muslim world, however, 'Christian' has an almost exclusively cultural, ethnic or political meaning. . . . Historic animosity over a thousand years (e.g., Christianity in light of the Crusades) taints the word 'Christian.'"[5]

In fact, some express the feeling that "Western Christians should be called *salibiyya*, 'Crusaderism,' as opposed to *masihiyya*, 'Christianity'. . . . Consequently, Western missionary activities [are] viewed by many as a kind of religious wedge used to break apart the culture of Islamic societies in order to make them more vulnerable to what was seen as the Western imperial crusade against Islam."[6] All of these issues were significant obstacles that Mazhar had to overcome before he could become "a pilgrim of Christ on the Muslim road." These are continuing obstacles that most of us in the West don't appreciate.

What Was Christ's Example?

In all of this Christ's approach was so different than ours often is. He didn't try and change a single person's culture. For the most part he meticulously avoided the political arguments of the day. He did defend the defenseless such as children or an alleged adulterous woman from religious leaders of the day. On the other hand, when confronted with the horribly unjust practices of the occupying Romans demanding that a Jew carry a soldier's load a mile, Jesus instructed them to "go the second mile." That sounded to the listeners as off the wall as telling a person today to double the amount the IRS said you owed and pay that to the government! When actually asked about paying taxes to an ungodly government he sidestepped the issue.[7] In fact, he was a master at sidestepping many political issues. More importantly, he did not try a change cultures.

The Apostle Paul took it a step further. A paraphrase of one passage of Scripture that he wrote might well read: "Let each person remain in the cultural situation that he or she is in. The culture that you are in is not the important thing but that you keep the commandments of God. If you are in an Eastern culture don't change to a Western culture; likewise if you are in a Western culture there is no need to change to an Eastern culture. Let each person remain in the culture that he or she is called in, being careful to follow the explicit commands of God."[8] We can conclude from this that we are not to attempt to change a culture but to help believers in other cultures to adapt the principles of Christ to their culture. In fact, the apostle Peter was reprimanded for failing to do this.[9]

Distinguishing between Western "Christian" Culture and Being Followers of Jesus

Years ago I attended a Communist-approved "Three Self Church" in China. Though I didn't understand a word of Chinese, I knew every word the choir was singing because the hymn was set to a Western tune. But when I heard music on the street, it wasn't Western—it was Chinese. I could cite the same phenomena in numerous countries around the world. We in the West have been oblivious to how we have commingled Western culture with our Christianity—to the detriment of God's truth and the people we encounter. Fortunately some of this is changing and there are now groups that encourage Christ-followers in every culture to express their faith through their own heart music and other arts.[10]

When we confuse Western culture with Christianity, we do a great disservice to the cause of Christ and the very people we want to influence. We put a giant barrier before every individual who otherwise might come into the kingdom of God from any other culture. In fact, when you stop and think about it, the culture of first-century Israel would hardly be recognizable by you and me today. Christ did not come to change culture—but to change individuals' and communities' lives. There is a giant difference!

Furthermore, it is not insignificant how the rest of the world sees the West with its violent and sexual media, its outright crime, and its frequent self-serving international pursuits. In fact, I would like to dissociate myself from a lot of Western culture.

E. Stanley Jones, a phenomenal missionary to India in the early twentieth century, is remembered for his interreligious lectures and influence on the Nehru family and Mahatma Gandhi. At one of his meetings, a Hindu lawyer asked:

> Do you mean to say . . . that you are not here to wipe out our civilization and replace it with your own? Do you mean that your message is Christ without any implications that we must accept Western civilization? I have hated Christianity, but if Christianity is Christ, I do not see how we Indians can hate it.[11]

At another meeting a Brahman said:

> "I don't like the Christ of your creeds and the Christ of your churches." My friend quietly replied, "Then how would you like the Christ of the Indian Road?" The Brahman thought a moment and pictured Christ in Indian garments, healing the sick, helping the poor and said: "I could love and follow the Christ of the Indian Road."[12]

Even Mahatma Gandhi's problem was not with Christ, but with us Christians. Once missionary E. Stanley Jones asked Gandhi:

> Mr. Gandhi, though you quote the words of Christ often, why is [it] that you appear to so adamantly reject becoming his follower? Gandhi replied, "Oh, I don't reject Christ. I love Christ. It's just that so many of you Christians are so unlike Christ. . . . If Christians would really live according to the teachings of Christ, as found in the Bible, all of India would be Christian today."[13]

We need to lovingly present Christ of the Indian road, the Muslim road, and the Asian road. He needs to be adorned with the culture and dress of the native region, but have the message of the carpenter from the ancient Palestinian city of Nazareth. Rick Wood, editor of *Mission Frontiers*, writes:

> The idea that a people must reject their own culture and join another's in order to fully obey and follow Jesus is one of the most foundational errors in mission strategy, and it is still going on today. Some still promote the belief that Muslims, Hindus, and Buddhists must reject all of their culture and join "ours" if they are to be true followers of Jesus.
>
> At issue is the foundational failure of the Church and some missionaries to separate their own culture from the gospel. This is not just a problem for people in the West. All cultures and peoples are prone to think that their culture's expression of the gospel is the correct one and should be the model

for followers of Jesus all over the world. . . . The gospel travels on the road of love and respect for the people and their culture.[14]

Dot Evert and her husband spent fifty years in ministry to Native Americans and international students. Dot writes:

[N]o culture may call another culture evil. Every culture has flaws and problems and certainly is not perfect. . . . The lesson of history is that when cultural outsiders come in and tell a people that everything in their culture is evil, then we are cutting them off from the grace of God and the power of the Holy Spirit to transform their lives and their culture at His direction. The gospel travels on the road of love and respect, not by coercion and force. . . . As long as obedience to the Word of God is the foundation, then we must allow Native peoples and people of all cultures to determine what forms and practices they choose to use in worshipping God.[15]

Thus, when you ask a Muslim or Hindu or someone of any other people group around the world to give up his or her culture in order to be a follower of Jesus, you are creating a giant unnecessary barrier. Mazhar Mallouhi affirms:

The word "Christian" can . . . carry very negative Western cultural connotations. As a result, accepting Christianity is seen by most Arab Muslims today as cultural destruction. True to form, much Western Christian mission activity has prescribed cultural disengagement and isolation for Muslims who wish to follow Christ.[16]

Christ did not tell the woman at the well to give up her Samaritan culture, nor did he tell the Roman centurion to keep the Jewish laws or to leave Caesar's ungodly army![17] He did tell the soldiers not to take things unlawfully, a principle that transcends all cultures because it is universally immoral.[18] He never tried to change people's cultures.

Some of the early missionaries had it right. E. Stanley Jones, in his seminal work, talked about "The Christ of the Indian Road." Hudson Taylor, while alienating himself from many of his fellow Westerners, took on Chinese dress, including wearing the customary queue.

Renowned missiologist Ralph D. Winter says:

> [W]hat very few congregations in America are prepared to understand is that dragging people out of their culture and converting them to what they think a "Christian" should look like is not what the Bible teaches. The Bible talks of our conveying a treasure in earthen vessels. The earthen vessels are not the important thing, but the treasure is. The new vessel will be another very different earthen vessel. This is what happened when the faith of the Bible was first conveyed to Greeks, In that case the treasure of biblical faith in an earthen Jewish vessel became contained in a Greek earthen vessel. Later it went to Latin vessels and to Germanic vessels and to English vessels and is now contained in Muslim vessels, Hindu vessels and Buddhist vessels. . . . Paul was very insistent that. . . . culture conversion was not necessary in becoming a follower of Christ.[19]

Mark Siljander in *A Deadly Misunderstanding* tells of two American aid workers in Afghanistan who had been arrested by the Taliban for allegedly "preaching Christianity" and who might get the death penalty. The article went on to quote a Taliban foreign minister as saying: "Jesus is highly regarded here, but Christianity is not."[20] We need to stop preaching Christianity, and not put down Islam or any other religion, but simply *to lift up Jesus.*[21] He has promised that if he is lifted up he will draw all people to himself.[22]

Conclusion

Obviously in some of this chapter I am using the term *Westernizing* and to some extent even *Christianizing* in a derogative way, particularly when we try and change cultures, to emphasize both to the Christian and the antagonist of Christianity that, unfortunately, Christian*ity* often has been and in *many ways* continues to be a negative factor in some individuals' minds and world history.[23]

Rick Wood takes it a step further saying: "It is also time for us to stop calling ourselves Christians . . . because . . . In the Muslim world the term comes with much negative baggage." Unfortunately, not only the Muslim culture but much of the world—including here in the West—has a negative impression of Christianity. Who we are and what we call ourselves will be the topic of the next several chapters.

Chapter 10

What Then Do We Do with This Man Called Jesus?

On April 13, 1970, Apollo 13 was 200,000 miles from the Earth heading for the moon when an in-flight explosion jeopardized the lives of the three astronauts. The world listened in horror to the now-famous words: "Houston, we have a problem."[1] That was putting it mildly—their very lives were in jeopardy.

We Have a Problem

You and I also face a major problem: What to do with Jesus? The most familiar verse in the Bible says that "God so loved the world that He gave His only begotten Son that whoever believes in Him should not perish but have everlasting life." Following this it says: "He who believes in Him is not condemned; *but he who does not believe is condemned already,* because he has not believed in the name of the only begotten Son of God."[2] Other passages declare that the pathway to God is exclusively through Christ. In fact, one verse referring to Christ reads, "Salvation comes no other way; no other name has been or will be given to us by which we can be saved."[3] In chapter 1, I quoted a verse in the Bible that states that God desires for all individuals to spend eternity in heaven. However, the very next verse makes the means very specific: "There is one God and one Mediator between God and men, the Man Christ Jesus."[4]

There is no question that these are audacious claims—Christ alleging not only to be equal with God, but also *the only* means to God and to the right to enjoy eternity in heaven. The Scriptures own the fact that this is a giant "stumbling block" to some and "foolishness" to others.[5] As C. S. Lewis has appropriately said, "Either this man was and is, the Son of God: or else a madman or something worse."[6] There is no middle ground. This is as big a problem for you and me as being in a space capsule with an explosion of one of our two oxygen tanks!

In previous chapters I made the case from Scriptures that individuals can and will be in heaven who have never heard of the name of Jesus. So how does one reconcile that conclusion with this claim that Christ is the only way to God?

What Did He Know, When Did He Know It, and What Did He Do about It?

Howard Baker, a U.S. senator from Tennessee, became famous during the Watergate Hearings by asking, "What did the president know and when did he know it?" In subsequent years numerous issues involving politics have arisen and the questions have been: "What did he know; when did he know it; and what did he do about it?"

These questions fit precisely for a person's knowledge about Jesus. It has appropriately been stated: "God will judge us according to our response to the knowledge we received."[7] The Scriptures inform us: "In the past God overlooked such ignorance, but now he commands all people everywhere to repent."[8] So the crucial issue, it seems to me, is whether or not an individual knows of Christ's provision for his or her sins and what he or she has done about it. This raises a logical question: "how much knowledge about Christ and his plan of salvation is necessary?" Clearly, I can't answer that, and no human can; God, the righteous judge, will make that determination.

Christ once asked his disciples, "Who do men say that I am?"[9] The disciples answered by saying that some thought he was John the Baptist, some thought he was Elijah, and others that he was Jeremiah or one of the prophets. In today's vernacular that would be like saying, "Jesus was a good man, a wonderful teacher, a charismatic leader, or a self-sacrificing idealist." Then Christ honed in on his disciples by asking them, "But who do you say that I am?" We are confronted with the same question today. Peter, who often responded impetuously, gave the right answer: "You are the Christ, the Son of the living God."[10] Later, Thomas got more specific, saying to Christ, "My Lord and my God."[11] Every person who has knowledge about Christ must answer this question, and the response determines one's eternal destiny. We will be judged on the basis of what we have known during our sojourn on earth and what we have done with that information. Erwin Lutzer, senior pastor of Moody Church in Chicago, elaborates: "They will be judged on the basis of what they did with what they knew, or should have known."[12]

Essentials for Salvation for the Person Who Knows about Christ

It seems to me, in carefully studying the Scriptures, that there are five essentials for *knowing* whether or not one is going to heaven *if one has knowledge about Christ*: (1) a sense of a personal need that springs from one's knowing that he or she doesn't measure up to God's perfect standards;[13] (2) a response to God's wooing with a deep faith in our sovereign God; (3) a realization that access to God is only through his Son, Jesus Christ;[14] (4) acknowledgement that Christ, though God, descended from heaven and was born, lived a sinless life, was crucified, died for our sins, rose from the dead, and ascended to heaven;[15] resulting in (5) repentance and a life that is transformed, thus giving evidence of a deep faith in God and his Son.[16]

I have been asked what does a "transformed life" look like? I am reluctant to try and answer this, as one really needs to consult the entire New Testament for an adequate answer. But I believe it will start with a trust and commitment to Christ. One's goal will be to have a life that is pleasing to God. The person will shun sin and endeavor to live a righteous life. Those around him or her should notice a significant and positive difference as a follower of Christ in comparison to the world at large. One will want to read the Scriptures and fellowship with other believers. A follower of Jesus will be concerned for the spiritual and physical needs of those around him or her.

In chapter 1, I stated that individuals can become right with God (justified) without ever knowing about Christ. They are, nevertheless saved through the redemptive work carried out for them by Christ, though they may never be aware of it in this life. He is the means of their eternal salvation. However, once an individual has knowledge of Christ, he or she must accept him as Lord and Savior, recognizing that he is the necessary mediator between a person and God.[17]

One Mediator

We now come to the conclusion that there is one mediator between God and human beings—Jesus Christ. The Scriptures make it exceedingly clear that he is the only, and necessary, go between. No church, no sacrament, no other human being is *essential* in your or my establishing a right relationship with God. For "God . . . desires all men to be saved and to come to the knowledge of the truth. For there is one God and one Mediator between God and men, the Man Christ Jesus."[18]

God Is the Behind-the-Scenes Initiator of Salvation

Though it may sometimes seem like we are the initiators in this whole process, actually God is the originator. He is behind the scenes encouraging us toward himself using sundry means such as the magnificence of nature or the marvels of our own bodies. He uses pain and suffering, friends, the printed page, and even religion. As we follow the wooing of his Spirit we will be given more truth.

The Seeker Will Be Given More Truth

We have already discussed how both the Ethiopian treasurer and the Roman centurion, who had a little knowledge of God but were honestly seeking truth, were, in fact, given more truth. More accurately we should say they were responding to God's nudging of their heart. I have heard recent stories of individuals in remote parts of the earth today seeking God's truth who subsequently have been given more truth. Furthermore, the Scriptures promise that those who seek God will find him when they seek him with all their heart.[19]

Saved People Will Always Respond Positively to the Claims of Christ

In addition, I believe we can conclude that those who have saving faith not knowing about Christ, as discussed in chapter 1, in fact have their salvation through the finished work of Christ and will, given the opportunity, always respond positively when they comprehend the claims of Christ. Theologians as early as Thomas Aquinas held to this position, and we see examples of this principle in the Scriptures.[20]

In fact, Honey II, whose belief in God I told you about in chapter 2, tore down his heathen idols only to have his daughter become deathly sick. He climbed a mountain to call out to God and his daughter was healed. He later walked miles and miles to find a Gospel of Mark and later became "a marvelous 'teller of the Good News.'"[21]

Conclusion

So what am I going to do with the audacious claim that Christ makes? Is he a madman or something worse, or is he in fact the only mediator to God? When you think about it, there really is no middle ground. That is a more important issue for you and me to deal with than the problem faced by the three astronauts in Apollo 13; it's not just a life and death issue—it's an eternity issue.

Chapter 11

Why Then Would You Ever Want to Send Missionaries?

If what I am postulating in this book is true, it might seem that Christianity has another question to answer: "If a person can be saved through general revelation, why would you ever send missionaries?"[1] This question is reinforced when some missionaries Westernize believers in other cultures, thus creating havoc for them and us.

Job-like Believers Are the Exception

Earlier in this book I went to great efforts to support my thesis that individuals throughout time who have never heard of Christ *can* be saved. However, the numbers who have been or are being saved by responding to God only through general revelation is impossible to say. The number of people such as Job, Noah, the Ethiopian eunuch, or the Roman Cornelius is probably minuscule as compared to the entire human race.[2] So, though our just God provides this avenue of salvation to everyone on earth, the actual number of those who have or will come to spend eternity in heaven through this means is possibly very small.[3] Therefore, this possibility should not alter our passion to share the good news around the world, and it certainly doesn't alter God's command to "go into all the world."[4] When God's truth is clearly and appropriately proclaimed by transformed lives with appropriate words, many more will respond to the claims of Christ. So what I am postulating in this book should not alter the call or need for missions one iota.[5] There is no question that when people are personally confronted with the good news communicated by a humble follower of Jesus without a lot of unnecessary baggage, that they are much more likely to respond to the message of salvation than they are by general revelation.

We must also note that the Ethiopian eunuch and Cornelius were contemporaries of Christ when he walked the earth and proclaimed the great commission. The fact that these two men had saving faith did not alter Christ's call to "go into all the world."

Another fact to consider is that the Ethiopian eunuch and Cornelius both had a very incomplete knowledge and faith. They both needed further enlightenment to more fully understand and walk in God's ways. People like Mr. Ni, discussed in chapter 2, who was anxiously waiting for God's truth, needed a Hudson Taylor to declare it to him.

Lest We Forget: Christianity Has Done a Lot of Good throughout the World

In an earlier chapter 1 was pretty hard on Christianity, pointing out many of the negative things Christians have done around the world in Christ's name. Christianity has gone as far as trying to change cultures, sometimes with the sword.

But there is another side that, in all fairness, I must bring out. Christians, including Christian missionaries, have done a tremendous amount of good. Often they have been leaders in establishing schools, including higher education around the world. Our early Ivy League colleges were established by Christians. They have fought infanticide and cannibalism. Christians started untold numbers of hospitals. Compassion and care for the mentally ill was primarily initiated by Christians. The rights of women have been championed. Followers of Christ fought against genital mutilation of girls. Christians were responsible for stopping foot binding in China. William Wilberforce and the missionary William Carey were leaders in the campaign against the Indian practice of Sati, in which the wife was placed alive on top of her recently deceased husband's funeral pyre (pile of wood) and the two were cremated together.[6] Though many Christians supported slavery, it was the Christian influence of William Wilberforce and a converted captain of a slave ship, John Newton, that ended slavery in the English Empire. Christianity is often at the forefront of helping the homeless and hungry, the widows and orphans, and of carrying out other philanthropic endeavors. Lamin Sanneh, a convert from Islam to Christianity and Professor of Missions, World Christianity and History at Yale Divinity School, asserts that the missionary movement, overall, has been a culture preserving movement.[7]

Furthermore, other religions have not been innocent of crimes against humanity. For example, the Muslims had a thriving slave trade from East Africa, and certainly the Jihad, the "holy war," is a distortion of the teachings of the Qur'an.

Even as I write these pages, child sacrifice is taking place in Ethiopia's primitive Omo River region. Infants and little children, who are born out of wedlock, have damaged genitals, or whose top baby teeth emerge before the bottom ones are considered *mingi,* or "cursed." The elders of the community believe that with every breath these little ones are beckoning an evil spirit into their village. Therefore, they are killed by drowning or by pouring sand into their mouth and throat. Through the influence of missionaries, Christians in the region, at great risk to themselves and their families, are doing their best to stop these child sacrifices.[8] We as Christians should continue to help the down and out, whether next door or halfway around the globe.

Not Westernizing or Christianizing but Becoming Followers of Jesus

In chapter 9, I emphasized that we should stop Christianizing the world. By that I mean we should not try and impose our mixture of Western culture, politics, and religion on others. I say this because it appears to me that we Christians often confuse culture and politics with faith. Rather, we need to focus on a far more difficult task—our personally becoming disciples of Jesus, exalting him, and not mixing it with our political or cultural bent. Nevertheless, as disciples of Jesus we will promote the welfare of every person God created.

I am reminded of Gandhi, who was drawn to the teachings of Jesus but was repulsed by how Christians failed to live out a Christ-like life. This should not be. One day E. Stanley Jones turned to Mahatma Gandhi and asked how Christianity might be naturalized in India: "He very gravely and thoughtfully replied: 'I would suggest, first, that all of you Christians, missionaries and all, must begin to live more like Jesus Christ.'"[9]

Mazhar Mallouhi says, "I came to the conclusion that Christ never intended to establish a new religion, but instead came to simply establish his life in and among us."[10] The Great Commission is not to go to the entire world and Christianize it—it is to go into the entire world as a practicing follower of Jesus and then to teach others how to be his followers also.

Christ told religious leaders who knew the Scriptures backwards and forwards, "You keep locking people out of the kingdom of heaven."[11] I sometimes think we do the same thing. In 1925 E. Stanley Jones wrote: "Christianity must be defined as Christ, not the Old Testament, not Western civilization, not even the system built around him in the West, but Christ himself and to be a Christian is to follow him. . . . I have dropped out the term 'Christianity' from my announcements (it isn't found in the Scriptures, is it?)."[12]

I know a number of individuals and some groups who prefer not to call themselves "Christians" because of all the baggage associated with the term; they prefer to be called "disciples of Jesus" or "followers of Jesus," which places the greater emphases on how we live out our lives as students of Jesus. In fact, when the term "Christian" was used in the Scriptures to characterize the followers of Christ, it was probably used in a derogative way. More often in the Scriptures we followers of Jesus are referred to as people of "the Way."[13] In the final analysis what we call ourselves is only somewhat important—but how we live is crucial.

Mazhar calls himself a "Pilgrim of Christ" and refuses "to get into theological arguments and is against pushing one system over another. . . . His focus is instead on the person of Jesus Christ and what Jesus means to him."[14] I think he has it right.

We can conclude by saying that our number one task is to be personal followers of Jesus, focusing first and foremost on how we are living out our lives of discipleship. Part of our being apprentices of Christ is to live a life like his that includes going into the entire world and sharing his good news. And in the words of St. Francis of Assisi: "Preach the Gospel at all times, and if necessary, use words."

Bangarraju is a wonderful example of this principle. He is an evangelist and church planter in India. In 1996 he started going to a community and living out a Christ-like life. He taught illiterate children in a makeshift school under a tree, never talking about his faith. He saw a medical need so arranged for weekly medical visits to the village. Only after a full year had passed did Bangarraju talk about source of his compassion— Jesus. Now a large proportion of the village follows Christ.[15]

Afterword

As I sit here at my computer I reminisce—what is life all about anyway? Why am I here? I'd swear the clock runs faster than it did a few years ago. I remember when I was young, a week seemed so long, and a year seemed forever, and four years of high school or college seemed like an eternity. Now the long years of training and even the practice of internal medicine and psychiatry seem almost a blur. And the ultimate questions persist: What in the world is life all about? Why am I here? What's next? Where am I going? For all of us such questions probe a tremendous amount of mystery.

Now in my late 70s, a month seems like a flicker in time; I walk around the block and a year is gone. When we all get to eternity our earthly time will seem like a vague memory. The Bible speaks about it being like a vapor of steam that appears for a moment and then is gone.

It seems to me our time on planet earth is in preparation for the life to come. For some reason my going out for football comes to mind. My freshman year of high school I signed up and appeared on the appropriate morning in late summer for training. We were all issued equipment; we blocked, tackled, and ran laps from 8 in the morning till 6 at night. At the end of the day we could virtually wring the sweat out of our jerseys, and the next day the locker room stank. The days were difficult and seemed endless while living through them; but in reality, the week went by very fast. This torturous week was called "hell week." That week determined whether you were on the team and what position you played.

Or life might be compared to the four years of college being the preparation that determines what one will do the rest of one's life. The Apostle Paul likens it to running in a race to win.[1] Whatever the comparison you choose, I postulate that it has parallels to life on earth and in eternity. Our lives on earth are preparatory for how we are going to spend eternity. As Erwin Lutzer says, *"this life is training for the next."*[2]

God continues to call people from all over the world who are willing to put their trust in him, follow him, and thereby enjoy eternity with him surrounded in unimaginable splendor. *That's what life is all about.*

I am reminded of Jilla, a young Iranian who was a fanatic Muslim. As a sixth grader she dedicated herself to Islam almost in a military style of allegiance. She hit herself till she bled; she fasted till she ended in the hospital; and she memorized the entire Qur'an. But she sensed something wasn't right in her personal faith. She wanted more of Allah. So she prayed, "Lord, God, I want to find You." Through a series of events and continually seeking the truth, she eventually found her Savior through a New Testament.[3]

Recently I heard an interview with Congressman Paul Broun, MD, from Georgia.[4] He told about being an atheist whose life was in shambles—several divorces and not knowing which way to turn. Then he remembered watching a professional football game and seeing behind the goal post an individual with rainbow dyed hair waving a banner with John 3:16 on it. I don't know about you, but though John 3:16 is one of the most cherished verses in the Bible to me, I get turned off by such a demonstration. Nevertheless, Doctor Paul Broun found a Gideon Bible and prayed, "God, if you are real—show me." He started reading it and his life was transformed.

God is drawing you to himself. He might be using the awareness that there must be an intelligent designer behind the cosmos and all that is in it. Or it might be the sense of "what is life all about?" or "what happens after death?" For some it might be the consciousness that there must be more to life than what you are experiencing, and for others it might be the conviction of unforgiven sin. Whatever the reason, I urge you to respond to the One who is actually wooing you to himself. You are promised, "If you seek Him, He will be found by you."[5] Dallas Willard comments:

> Multitudes of people have come to full knowledge of God because in a moment of complete hopelessness they prayed "The Atheist's Prayer" or something like it: "O God, if there is a God, save my soul if I have a soul." When that is the true cry of the heart, of the inmost spirit of the individual, who has no longer any hope other than God, God hears and responds without fail. It is as if he has a "heart monitor" installed in every person. And when the heart truly reaches out to God *as* God, no longer looking to itself or others, he responds with the gift of "life from above."[6]

103

Don't take my word for all of this—*it is much too important for that*. Respond to God's pursuit of you. I suggest beginning by reading the third and fourth books in the New Testament, the Gospels of Luke and John, for the best overview of Jesus. Continue your reading by tackling the first six books in the New Testament as a good overview of its content. Then read the entire New Testament. As you go, ask God to reveal himself to you. Other pilgrims can be a tremendous help, but you must be careful—some will facilitate your progress, others may actually complicate it. The gold standard is always the Scriptures.

In December 1999 Billy Graham told the following story before the United Nations:

> I'm reminded today of Albert Einstein, the great physicist who this month has been honored by *Time* magazine as the Man of the Century. Einstein was once traveling from Princeton on a train when the conductor came down the aisle, punching the tickets of every passenger. When he came to Einstein, Einstein reached in his vest pocket. He couldn't find his ticket, so he reached in his trouser pockets. It wasn't there, so he looked in his briefcase but couldn't find it. Then he looked in the seat beside him; he still couldn't find it.
>
> The conductor said, "Dr. Einstein, I know who you are. We all know who you are. I'm sure you bought a ticket. Don't worry about it."
>
> The conductor continued down the aisle punching tickets. As he was ready to move to the next car, he turned around and saw the great physicist down on his hands and knees looking under his seat for his ticket. The conductor rushed

back and said, "Dr. Einstein, Dr. Einstein, don't worry. I know who you are. No problem. You don't need a ticket. I'm sure you bought one."

Einstein looked at him and said, "Young man, I too know who I am. What I don't know is where I'm going."

It has been reported that Dr. Graham more recently said: See the suit I'm wearing? It is a brand new suit. My children and my grandchildren are telling me I've gotten a little slovenly in my old age. I used to be a bit more fastidious. So I bought a new suit for this luncheon and one more occasion. You know what that occasion is?

This is the suit in which I'll be buried. But when you hear I'm dead, I don't want you to immediately remember the suit I'm wearing. I want you to remember this: I not only know who I am . . . I know where I'm going.[7]

Life is short and I trust you also know where you are going. In the words of the song: "This world is not my home, I'm just a passing through."[8] The Scriptures say: "I write this to you that believe in the name of the Son of God; that you may know that you have eternal life."[9]

The introduction to this book raised the question of whether we have a stingy or a generous God. I conclude we have an extremely generous God who desires that you spend eternity with him in the splendors of heaven. He has and will continue to take the initiative, and I pray that you will respond to his nudging so that you can be certain of your eternal future.

Acknowledgements

I am deeply indebted to many individuals for making this book possible. Foremost is my wife, Betty, who patiently endured my combing over Scriptures, reading numerous books, and spending untold hours at the computer—thank you. Thanks to my daughter Susan Carlson Wood, who edited the manuscript and added her valuable perspective.

A number of individuals read this manuscript and gave their very helpful insights. But before I list them I need to tell you that some were enthusiastic about the book, and at least one suggested that maybe I shouldn't publish it; others had specific area(s) of concern—thus, thanking them for their helpful comments doesn't necessarily mean they endorsed all the contents of the book. Nevertheless, I heartily want to thank each of them for their constructive suggestions—the ones I didn't follow I take full responsibility for: Chris and Patti Appel, George Caudle, Gordon Kirk, Ed Lassiter, Tim Miller, Cal Milnes, Paul Pierson, George Samuel, Bart Tarman, and my Saturday morning men's study group. I want to especially thank Paul Pierson, PhD, dean emeritus of Fuller's School of World Mission. He reviewed this manuscript twice and wrote detailed suggestions, "like [he was] reviewing a masters or doctorate thesis"; most of which I have incorporated into the book.

Last, but not least, I want to thank those who were willing to write statements about this book: Joe Handley, Herbert Hoefer, John Huffman, Gary Moon, Paul Pierson and Dallas Willard. I wanted to have comments from Evangelicals but am aware that many in that camp will struggle with some of the assertions I put forth in this book. Therefore, if you have trouble with any of the contents of this book—blame me and not those who were kind enough to make a statement about this book.

Endnotes

Preface

1   J. B. Phillips, *Your God Is Too Small* (New York: Macmillan, 13th printing, 1957), pp. 37-40, italics in original.

2   John Sanders, *No Other Name: An Investigation into the Destiny of the Unevangelized* (Eugene, OR: Wipf and Stock, 2001), p. 23.

3   Ibid., p. 20.

4   Terrance L. Tiessen, *Who Can Be Saved? Reassessing Salvation in Christ and World Religions* (Downers Grove, IL: InterVarsity Press, 2004), p. 126.

5   I am using the word *saved*, meaning "saved from hell and going to heaven," and the word *heaven* interchangeably throughout the book.

6   Jn 5:39; 14:26; Acts 17:11.

7   1 Jn 2:27.

8   Richard J. Mouw, "An Open-Handed Gospel," *Christianity Today*, April 2008, p. 46.

Chapter 1

1   Job 1:1. Job and his four counselors lived in the land of Uz. No one knows just where Uz is located and how they came about their understanding of God.

2   Job 42:9; see also 2:3; 19:25-26. Job's righteousness is verified in Ezek 14:14 and Jas 5:11.

3   Biblical examples are often referred to as "holy pagans." Examples typically given are Abel, Enoch, Noah, Job, Melchizedek, Jethro, Abimelech, Naaman, and some would include Abraham. Some would question calling them "holy pagans or heathen," but I believe this is appropriate for as far as we know general revelation initially drew them to God before there was a tangible, visual, or verbal special manifestation by God.

4   Josh 2:1-24; 6:22-23, 25; Mt 1:5; Heb 11:31; Jas 2:25.

5   See entire book of Jonah; Mt 12:41; Lk 11:32.

6   Gen 4:4; Mt 23:35; Heb 11:4.

7   Gen 6:8-9; 7:1.

8   Mt 2:1-12.

9   Lk 23:43.

10 Mt 8:10.

11 Acts 8:26-40.

12 Acts 10:1-43, italics added. Some argue that Cornelius wasn't saved at this time and was only saved after Peter spoke to him because verse 43 says, "whoever believes in Him *will* receive remission of sins." However, in verse 35 Peter has previously said, "whoever fears Him and works righteousness *is* accepted by Him." Terrance L. Tiessen supports this understanding, stating that Aquinas, Calvin, Edwards, Morgan, and Ronald Nash all indicate Cornelius was saved before he became a "Christian." *Who Can Be Saved? Reassessing Salvation in Christ and World Religions* (Downers Grove, IL: InterVarsity Press, 2004), p. 178.

13 Gen 18:25.

14 John Sanders says, "Are all the 'heathen' lost? Is there an opportunity for those who have never heard of Jesus to be saved? . . . is the most-asked apologetic question on U.S. college campuses." John Sanders, ed., *What about Those Who Have Never*

Heard? Three Views on the Destiny of the Unevangelized (Downers Grove, IL: IVP Academic, 1995), p. 7.

15 C. S. Lewis, *Mere Christianity* (Great Britain: Fontana Books, 1952), p. 62.

16 J. I. Packer, *God's Words: Studies of Key Bible Themes* (Grand Rapids, MI: Baker Book House, 1981), p. 210.

17 Alister E. McGrath, "A Particularist View: A Post-Enlightenment Approach," in *Four Views on Salvation in a Pluralistic World*, ed. Dennis L. Okholm and Timothy R. Phillips (Grand Rapids, MI: Zondervan, 1995), p. 178, italics added.

18 Acts 10:34-35.

19 Rom 2:6-13 says the doers of the law shall be justified. See also Lk 19:1-10; Jn 8:39; Rom 4; Gal 3:6; Jas 2:14-26.

20 A few representative verses about *personal need*:
> Isa 59:2: "[Y]our iniquities have separated you from your God; And your sins have hidden His face from you, So that He will not hear."
> Eccl 7:20: "There is not a just man on the earth who . . . doesn't sin."
> Isa 53:6: "All we like sheep have gone astray."
> Isa 66:2: "But on this one will I look, even to him that is poor and of a contrite spirit."
> Rom 3:23: "for all have sinned and fall short of the glory of God." I am aware that this verse is from the New Testament but I believe it is applicable throughout time.

21 A few representative verses on *seeking God*:
> Deut 4:29: "you will seek the LORD your God, and you will find Him, if you seek Him with all your heart and with all your soul."
> 2 Chr 15:1-15, esp. vv. 2, 4, 15: "If you seek me you will find me."
> Prov 8:17: "those who seek me diligently will find me."
> Isa 55:6-7: "Seek the LORD while He may be found, Call

upon Him while He is near. Let the wicked forsake his way. And the unrighteous man his thoughts; Let him return to the Lord, And He will have mercy on him; And to our God, For He will abundantly pardon."

Jer 29:13: "you will seek Me and find Me, when you search for Me with all your heart."

Joel 2:32 and Acts 2:21: "Whoever calls on the name of the LORD shall be saved."

Jn 9:31: "Now we know that God does not hear sinners; but if anyone is a worshiper of God and does His will He hears him."

1 Pet 3:12: "For the eyes of the Lord are on the righteous, and His ears are open to their prayers."

22 A few representative verses on *belief*:

Jonah 3:5: "So the people of Nineveh believed God".

Gen 15:6: "And he (Abraham) *believed* in the Lord and He accounted it to him for righteousness." The passage is repeated in Gal 3:6.

23 A few representative verses on *repentance*:

Jonah 3:8-9: "let every one turn from his evil way. . . . Who can tell if God will turn and relent . . . so that we may not perish?"

Ezek 14:6: "Thus says the LORD God: 'Repent, turn away from your idols and turn your faces away from all your abominations.'" See also Ezek 18:30-32.

24 Some representative verses teaching that *our life will evidence our faith:*

Gen 7:1: "I have seen that you are righteous before Me in this generation."

Gen 26:5: God looked favorably on Abraham because he "*obeyed* My voice and kept My charge, My commandments."

2 Kings 5:1-19: Naaman, commander of the army of the

king of Syria, clearly sought after the true God and had faith and obedience to be healed. (Many New Testament verses demonstrate that there is often a relationship between being healed and being saved. See, for example, Mt 9:2-5; Mk 2:1-10).

Job 1:1: "Job was blameless, upright and feared God and shunned evil."

Acts 10:34-35: "I now realize how true it is that God does not show favoritism but accepts men from every nation who fear him and do what is right."

Mic 6:8: "And what does the LORD require of you But to do justly, To love mercy, And to walk humbly with your God?"

25 Don Richardson says, "there are also more than 300 declarative passages in the Old Testament which amplify God's oath-sealed promise to bless all nations on Earth." *Eternity in Their Hearts* (Ventura, CA: Regal Books, 1981, 2005), p. 143.

26 Ex 9:16; Gen 12:2-3 NIV, italics added.

27 Ps 34:18.

28 Ps 51:17.

29 Ps 67:2, 4, 7, italics added.

30 Ps 34:22.

31 Ps 86:5, italics added.

32 Jn 10:16.

33 Prov 8:17; Joel 2:32, italics added.

34 Rev 5:9: "redeemed us . . . out of every nation, tribe and tongue and people"; see also Rev 7:9: "a great multitude which no one could number, of all nations, tribes, peoples, and tongues, standing before the throne and before the Lamb, clothed with white robes."

35 See, for example, "List of Languages by Time of Extinction," Wikipedia (last modified November 12, 2010), http://

en.wikipedia.org/wiki/List_of_languages_by_time_of_
extinction#2nd_millennium_BC.

36 Ps 53:2; Heb 11:6.

37 1 Tim 2:4.

38 Lk 12:48; Rom 2:12.

39 William A. Dembski and Michael R. Licona, eds., *Evidence
for God* (Grand Rapids, MI: Baker Books, 2010), p. 198, italics
in original. Note copyright by the Southern Baptist North
American Mission Board.

40 *Webster's College Dictionary* (New York: Random House, 1995),
defines *heathen* as "an unconverted individual of a people that
do not acknowledge the God of the Bible or of the Koran . . .
uncultured, or uncivilized . . . pagan . . . applied to peoples
who are not Christian, Jewish or Muslim . . . often used of
those whose religion is unfamiliar and therefore regarded as
primitive, unenlightened, or uncivilized." It defines *pagan* as "one
. . . observing a polytheistic religion . . . a person who is not a
Christian, Jew, or Muslim; heathen."

41 Jn 10:16.

42 William Barclay, *The Gospel of Matthew*, vol. 2, rev. ed.
(Louisville, KY: Westminster John Knox, 1975), p. 291.

43 Acts 10:24-45.

44 Num 11:25-29.

45 1 Kings 19:10-18.

46 Mk 9:38-40; Lk 9:49-54.

47 Acts 10:35, italics added.

48 See 3 John 9.

49 Mt 8:11-12; Lk 13:28.

50 Lk 15:28-32; Mt 7:1-5; also Mt 15:21-28; Mk 9:38-40; 10:13-14;
Lk 18:15-17; Jn 4:27.

51 Personal paraphrase of Jn 3:16-17.

52 I take this idea from what John Wesley said about George Whitefield, two great English evangelists who disagreed sharply on some doctrinal matters. Wesley was asked if he expected to see Whitefield in heaven. He said "no." The questioner then responded, "Then you do not think Whitefield is a converted man?" To which Wesley is reported to have said: "Of course he is a converted man! But I do not expect to see him in heaven—because he will be so close to the throne of God and I so far away that I will not be able to see him!" From: Warren W. Wiersbe, *Be Joyful* (Colorado Springs, Colo.: Chariot Victor, 1974), p. 43.

53 All of us are warned about not adding or taking away from the Scriptures and the consequences thereof. See Rev 22:18. Clearly, some groups add or subtract a lot more than others, and God will hold them responsible for that. Furthermore, the further one's addition is from God's truth the more it will obscure God's message of salvation.

54 Paul made a point that he didn't come to baptize. See 1 Cor 1:17.

55 Robert L. Millet, *A Different Jesus? The Christ of the Latter-Day Saints* (Grand Rapids, MI: Eerdmans, 2005), p. 80.

56 Ibid., pp. 112, 176-77.

57 Ibid., p. xii.

58 Ibid., p. 183, italics added.

Chapter 2

1 Bilquis Sheikh, with Richard H. Schneider, *I Dared to Call Him Father: The Miraculous Story of a Muslim Woman's Encounter with God* (Grand Rapids, MI: Chosen Books, 2003).

2 Mark A. Gabrel, *Islam and Terrorism* (Lake Mary, FL: Charisma House, 2002), pp. 16-19.

3 Rick Wood, editorial comment: "Muslim, Hindu and Buddhist Followers of Jesus: How Should We Respond?" *Mission*

Frontiers (The U.S. Center for World Missions) 33:3, May-June 2011, p. 4.

4 Personal communication, June 15, 2011.

5 "Muslim Followers of Jesus," *Christianity Today*, December 2009, pp. 32-35.

6 Mk 14:66-72; I am aware of verses like Mt 10:32-33; Lk 12:8-9; Rom 10:9; and 1 Jn 4:15 that strongly encourage confessing Christ. Furthermore, Mt 10:33 and Lk 12:9 do indicate that denial of Christ will result in denial before God or his angels.

7 Josh 6:17.

8 Jn 3:1-9; 7:50-51; 19:39; 2 Kings 5:1-19.

9 Paul-Gordon Chandler, *Pilgrims of Christ on the Muslim Road* (Lanham, MD: Cowley Publications, 2007), p. 21.

10 Paul-Gordon Chandler, "Can a Muslim Be a Follower of Christ?" *Mission Frontiers,* July-August 2008, p. 12.

11 Kevin Greesan, "Church Planting Movements among Muslim Peoples," *Mission Frontiers,* March-April 2011, pp. 22-24.

12 Krikor Markarian, "Today's Iranian Revolution: How the Mullahs Are Leading the Nation to Jesus," *Mission Frontiers*, September-October 2008, pp. 6-13.

13 J. Dudley Woodberry, "Muslim Missions: Then & Now," *Christianity Today,* September 8, 2011, p. 1, http://www.christianitytoday.com/ct/article_print.html?id=93506.

14 For further discussion on this, see Miroslav Volf, *Allah: A Christian Response* (New York: HarperOne, 2011).

15 1 Sam 16:7.

16 2 Chr 16:8-9 TLB.

17 Carl Medearis, *Muslims, Christians and Jesus* (Bloomington, MN: Bethany House, 2008), p. 30; Rick Brown, "Who Was 'Allah' before Islam? Evidence that the Term 'Allah' Originated with

Jewish and Christian Arabs" in *Toward Respectful Understanding & Witness Among Muslims*, Edited by Evelyne A. Reisacher (Pasadena, CA, William Carey Library 2012), pp. 147-178.

18 Mark D. Siljander, *A Deadly Misunderstanding: A Congressman's Quest to Bridge the Muslim-Christian Divide* (New York: HarperCollins, 2008), p. 183.

19 See, for example, Gen 15:1; 26:24; 28:12-17; Mt 1:20-21; 2:13; Acts 9:1-19, etc.

20 Acts 2:17.

21 Peter Bruce [pen name], "His Kingdom Coming to Afghanistan?" *Mission Frontiers*, September-October 2010, pp. 28-30.

22 J. Dudley Woodberry and Russell G. Shubin, "Why I Chose Jesus," *Mission Frontiers*, no date given, p. 5, http://www.missionfrontiers.org/2001/01/muslim.htm, as quoted in Tiessen, *Who Can Be Saved?* p. 180.

23 Tim Stafford, "India's Grassroots Revival," *Christianity Today*, July 8, 2011, p. 7, http://christianitytoday.com/ct/article_print.html?id=92825.

24 Gal 3:28 NLT.

25 Herbert E. Hoefer, *Churchless Christianity* (Pasadena, CA: William Carney Library, 2001), pp. xi-xx.

26 E. Stanley Jones, *The Christ of the Indian Road* (New York: Abingdon, 1925), p. 64.

27 Hoefer, *Churchless Christianity*, pp. 17, 23, 42.

28 Ibid., p. 106.

29 Ibid., pp. 198-99, italics added.

30 Wood, editorial comment, pp. 4-5.

31 Gavriel Gefen, "Jesus Movements: Discovering Biblical Faith in the Most Unexpected Places," *Mission Frontiers* (The U.S. Center for World Missions) 33:3, May-June 2011, p. 7.

32 Ibid., p. 8.

33 Ibid., pp. 9-10.

34 See the entire May-June 2011 edition of *Mission Frontiers* (The U.S. Center for World Missions) 33:3.

35 Dallas Willard, *The Divine Conspiracy* (San Francisco: HarperSanFrancisco, 1998), pp. 32-33, italics in original. He quotes from Ps 34:18 and Rom 10:12.

36 Dr. and Mrs. Howard Taylor, *Hudson Taylor's Spiritual Secret* (Chicago: Moody Press, 2009), p. 94.

37 Ibid., pp. 94-95.

38 See endnote 52 in chapter 1.

39 Edith Schaeffer, *Affliction: A Compassionate Look at the Reality of Pain and Suffering* (Grand Rapids, MI: Baker Books, 1978, 1993), pp. 124-25.

40 Ibid., p. 125.

41 Mt 25:31-46: For further elaboration on many of the issues discussed in chapter 1 and 2 of this book, see Sir Norman Anderson, *Christianity and World Religions* (Leicester, England, Inter-Varsity Press, 1970, 1984).

Chapter 3

1 Clearly, it is not my place, or probably any one's place to judge any specific individual and how they stand before God Almighty. However, when you compare their lives with the Scriptures it *seems* very apparent that these men fit the belief system and life style that both God and Christ condemned. Could they have had a death bed conversion? One cannot be sure but Scriptures suggest that individuals like this have grieved God's Spirit to such extent that He no longer draws them to Himself and thus their fate is sealed.

2 2 Sam 3:39.

3 "Summary of Key Findings," Pew Forum on Religion and Public

Life, U.S. Religious Landscape Survey 2008, http://religions .pewforum.org/pdf/report2religious-landscape-study-key-findings.pdf.

4   From a *U.S. News and World Report* survey dated 1997, as cited by John Ortberg, *It All Goes Back in the Box* (Grand Rapids, MI: Zondervan, 2007), pp. 120-21.

5   Luke 13:23-25 TLB.

6   Mt 7:13-14; see also Mt 22:14; Lk 13:23-29. B. B. Warfield calls this the "dogma of the fewness of the saved," as cited in Terrance L. Tiessen, *Who Can Be Saved? Reassessing Salvation in Christ and World Religions* (Downers Grove, IL: InterVarsity Press, 2004), p. 289.

7   Isa 10:22; Rom 9:27 NIV. Mt 8:10-12 indicates that many individuals from around the world will be in heaven while many Jews will not be there.

8   William Barclay, *The Gospel of Matthew*, vol. 2, rev. ed. (Louisville, KY: Westminster John Knox, 1975), p. 283.

9   Lk 3:8.

10   *Webster's College Dictionary* (New York: Random House, 1995), p. 1012.

11   Mt 23:25-28; Lk 11:39.

12   Mt 7:22-23 says: "Many will say to Me in that day, Lord, Lord, have we not prophesied in Your Name . . . and done many wonders in Your name? And then I will declare to them, 'I never knew you: depart from Me, you who practice lawlessness!'"

13   Timothy Keller, *The Prodigal God: Recovering the Heart of the Christian Faith* (New York: Dutton, 2008), p. 45, italics added.

14   Ibid., pp. 66-67.

Chapter 4

1   I am only responding to one aspect of Rob Bell's book. For a more comprehensive evaluation and rebuttal see Mark Galli's

book *God Wins: Heaven, Hell, and Why the Good News Is Better than Love Wins* (Carol Stream, IL: Tyndale House, 2011).

2　Rob Bell, *Love Wins: A Book about Heaven, Hell, and the Fate of Every Person Who Ever Lived* (New York: HarperOne, 2011), pp. 97-98, italics in original.

3　Gen 18:14.

4　Jer 32:17, 27.

5　Tit 1:2.

6　Lk 13:34; 19:41.

7　Jn 3:16; Prov 6:16; Isa 61:8; Amos 5:21.

8　1 Tim 2:4.

9　Jn 3:36.

Chapter 5

1　Prov 23:18.

2　This statement is generally attributed to Blaise Pascal, although the exact source is debated.

3　Augustine, *Confessions* 1.1.1 (397 AD).

4　"Summary of Key Findings," Pew Forum on Religion and Public Life, U.S. Religious Landscape Survey 2008, http://religions .pewforum.org/pdf/report2religious-landscape-study-key-findings.pdf.

5　Carlos Eire, *A Brief History of Eternity* (Princeton, NJ: Princeton University Press, 2010), pp. 201-4.

6　Ps 19:1 NIV; see also Acts 14:16-17.

7　Eccl 3:11.

8　Acts 14:17 and Rom 1:19-21 NASB; see also all of Romans 1 and 2.

9　Don Richardson, *Eternity in their Hearts* (Ventura, CA: Regal Books, 1981, 2005); see back cover.

10   Richardson, *Eternity in their Hearts*, p. 140.

11   Rodney Stark, *Discovering God* (New York: HarperCollins, 2007), pp. 23, 58, 62.

12   Rom 2:14-16 MSG.

13   Heb 9:27NIV.

14   Rom 14:12 NIV; Acts 24:15; see also Acts 17:30-31; 2 Cor 5:10.

15   Randy Alcorn, *Heaven* (Carol Stream, IL: Tyndale House, 2004), p. 47.

16   Mt 25:46; Jn 5:28-29; Acts 24:15; Rev 21:27.

17   As discussed in chapter 1 and will be elaborated on in greater detail later in the book.

18   Jn 5:29; see also Mt 13:47-50; 25:31-34; and Dan 12:2, which says: "And *many* of them that sleep in the dust of the earth shall awake, *some* to everlasting life, and *some* to shame and everlasting contempt." Italics added.

19   1 Cor 15:53 TLB; see also Rom 2:6-7; 2 Cor 5:1-8. Many passages speak of obtaining eternal life, such as, "And this is the way to have eternal life, by knowing you [God]" (Jn 17:3 TLB). These indicate that through a right relationship with God we have eternal life or immortality.

20   1 Cor 13:12; see also 1 Cor 2:9.

21   For an excellent book on the subject, see Alcorn, *Heaven*.

22   Some verses suggesting rewards in heaven: Mt 16:27; 19:25-30; 20:21-28; 25:14-30; Lk 16:1-31; 19:12-19; Rom 2:1-13; 1 Cor 3:15; 2 Cor 5:9-10; 2 Tim 2:12; 4:6-8; Jas 1:12; Rev 2:9-10, 17, 23, 26; 3:2, 5, 21; 7:13-17; 20:11-15; 21:1-8; 22:12-19.

23   Robert Ervin Hough, *The Christian after Death* (Chicago: Moody Press, 1947), p. 82.

24   Alcorn, *Heaven*, p. 68.

25   John Piper, *Future Grace* (Sisters, OR: Multnomah Press, 1995), p. 364; verses that follow this quote include 1 Cor 3:8; Eph 6:8; 1 Thess 1:3; 2 Thess 1:11; Lk 19:12-27, and the Parable of the Talents.

26   There are certainly some strong verses on hell in the Scriptures, such as Mt 8:12; 13:42; 22:13; Lk 16:22-24; Rev 14:9-11; 20:7-10.

27   William V. Crockett, "The Metaphorical View," in *Four Views on Hell*, ed. William Crockett, series ed. Stanley N. Gundry (Grand Rapids, MI: Zondervan, 1996), pp. 43-76.

28   Edward William Fudge and Robert A. Peterson, *Two Views of Hell* (Downers Grove, IL: IVP Academic, 2000), p. 20.

29   Verses indicating hell is prepared for Satan and his angelic followers: Isa 14:12-15; Mt 25:41; 2 Pet 2:4; Rev 20:10-15.

30   Erwin W. Lutzer, *Your Eternal Reward* (Chicago: Moody Press, 1998), p. 12.

31   Crockett, "Metaphorical View," p. 74.

32   Lk 12:2-3.

33   Lk 12:47-48.

34   Some verses indicating varying degrees of punishment in hell: Mt 10:15; 11:22-24; 12:33-37; 23:33; 24:14; 25:14-46; 26:41; Lk 10:12-16; 12:46-48; 20:47; Rom 2:2-11; Jas 5:1-6; 2 Pet 2:21; Rev 20:11-14.

35   Lutzer, *Your Eternal Reward*, p. 167.

36   The Bible teaches that some things are revealed in greater clarity than others; this is one that the Scriptures do not elaborate on. See 1 Cor 13:12.

37   Edward William Fudge, in Fudge and Peterson, *Two Views of Hell*, p. 21.

38   Lk 12:4-5.

39 Verses that suggest endless torment in hell: Mt 25:41, 46; Mk 9:43-47; Rev 20:10.

40 Ps 37:2, 9-10, 20, 38; Rom 6:16-23; Phil 3:19; 2 Thess 1:9; Rev 20:14-15. There are many verses that contrast "everlasting life" with those dying, perishing, or destroyed, such as Jn 3:15-18, 36; Lk 13:3.

41 Robert A. Peterson, in Fudge and Peterson, *Two Views of Hell*, p. 94. Clark H. Pinnock says, "Maybe there will be a period of punishment before oblivion and nonbeing" ("The Conditional View," in *Four Views on Hell*, ed. William Crockett, series ed. Stanley N. Gundry [Grand Rapids, MI: Zondervan, 1996], p. 154).

42 Edward William Fudge, in Fudge and Peterson, *Two Views of Hell*, pp. 22, 185, 187.

43 John Stott, quoted in James I. Packer, "Evangelical Annihilationism in Review," *Reformation & Revival* 6, no. 2, Spring 1997, p. 48. Available at http://www.theologicalstudies .org.uk/pdf/ref-rev/06-2/6-2_packer.pdf.

44 Roger E. Olson, *The Mosaic of Christian Belief: Twenty Centuries of Unity & Diversity* (Downers Grove, IL: InterVarsity Press, 2002), p. 329.

45 There are a number of verses that clearly indicate that after death it will be too late to make a decision for Christ (see Lk 13:22-27; 16:19-31). Roman Catholics include intertestamental literature (Apocrypha) in their Bibles, not part of the cannon of Jewish or Protestant versions of the Bible, to support their position on purgatory. Even if one accepts these books and verses like 2 Macc 12:43-45, I do not find them convincing. See "Purgatory," (Robert H. Brom, Bishop of San Diego, August 10, 2004), on the Catholic Answers website: http://www.catholic.com/library/ purgatory.asp.

46 Jn 5:25-29; Acts 17:31; 2 Tim 4:8; 1 Pet 3:18–4:6; 1 Jn 4:17.

47 Josh 24:15; Heb 9:27; Lk 16:19-31; see also Mt 25:1-12.

48 Lk 13:23-29.

49 2 Cor 6:2 KJV.

Chapter 6

1 John R. Franke, "The Truth, and the Life," *Christianity Today*, December 2009, pp. 27-31.

2 See Acts 3:17; 17:30; 1 Tim 1:13.

3 Acts 15; Gal 2–3.

4 A. W. Tozer, *Born after Midnight* (Harrisburg, PA: Christian Publications, 1959), pp. 76, 79.

5 Gal 2:14-17.

6 Rom 11:33.

7 1 Cor 7:40.

8 1 Cor 13:9-12.

9 2 Chr 16:9; Prov 8:17; Jer 29:13; Acts 2:21.

10 Bruce L. Shelly, *Church History in Plain Language*, updated 2nd ed. (Nashville: Thomas Nelson, 1995), p. 75, italics added.

11 Acts 15:1-21.

12 2 Cor 11:3.

13 Acts 4:12; 1 Tim 2:5.

14 Christopher J. H. Wright, "Salvation Belongs to Our God," *Evangelical Interfaith Dialogue* Issue 1.4, Fall 2010, p. 4, italics added.

15 Lesslie Newbigin, "The Basis, Purpose and Manner of Inter-Faith Dialogue," *Scottish Journal of Theology* 30 (1977): 3. As quoted in Wright, "Salvation Belongs to Our God," p. 4.

16 2 Pet 3:9.

17 1 Tim 2:4.

18 Don Richardson, *Eternity in their Hearts* (Ventura, CA: Regal Books, 1981, 2005), cover.

19 Mary Joni Harris, "Straying from the Buddhist Path—Why I Stopped Following Buddha and Started Following Jesus" (AIIA Institute, copyright 2003, 2004), www.christiananswers.net/q-aiia/aiia-buddhism-harris.html.

20 Mt 23:13.

21 Gal 5:5-6 MSG.

Chapter 7

1 "Sacraments of the Catholic Church," Catholic Online, 2011, http://www.catholic.org/clife/prayers/sacrament.php.

2 John E. Phelen Jr., "Film and Book Reviews," *The Covenant Companion*, January 2011, p. 26.

3 Carlos Eire, *A Brief History of Eternity* (Princeton, NJ: Princeton University Press, 2010), p. 107, italics in original.

4 William Barclay, *The Gospel of Matthew*, vol. 2, rev. ed. (Louisville, KY: Westminster John Knox, 1975), p. 284.

5 Mt 19:16-30, italics added; see also Mk 10:17-22; Lk 18:18-23.

6 Eph 2:8-9.

7 Mt 19:25.

8 1 Cor 13:3.

9 Some verses that indicate our good works, no matter how good, will never get us into heaven: Isa 64:6; Mt 7:22-23; Mk 10:24; Lk 18:9-14; Rom 3:19-26; 9:30-33; Gal 2:16; 3:1-14, 26; Eph 2:8-9; Titus 3:4-7; Jas 2:10.

Chapter 8

1 Jas 2:14-26.

2 C. S. Lewis, *Mere Christianity* (London: Fontana Books, 1952), p. 156.

3   F. F. Bruce, *The Canon of Scripture* (Downers Grove, IL: InterVarsity Press, 1988), p. 243.

4   Jas 2:17.

5   Dallas Willard, *The Divine Conspiracy: Rediscovering Our Hidden Life in God* (New York: HarperCollins, 1998), p. 43, italics added.

6   Personal tally reading through the Gospels. See Jn 17:20; Mk 5:34.

7   Jn 8:11; Mk 8:34.

8   Mt 7:17-18; Lk 6:43-45; Rom 12:1-2.

9   Roger E. Olson, professor of theology at Baylor University, says: "According to all major Christian traditions over two thousand years of reflection and proclamation, personal salvation is both *gift* and *task.*" *The Mosaic of Christian Belief: Twenty Centuries of Unity & Diversity* (Downers Grove, IL: InterVarsity Press, 2002), p. 267.

10   2 Cor 5:17.

11   See Mt 7:20-21; Titus 1:16; Jas 2; 1 Jn 2:3-7; 3:10-24.

12   Mt 7:17-18; Lk 6:43.

13   Mt 7:21.

14   1 Jn 3:10.

15   Martin Luther's Definition of Faith: An excerpt from "An Introduction to St. Paul's Letter to the Romans," Luther's German Bible of 1522 by Martin Luther, 1483-1546, translated by Rev. Robert E. Smith from *Dr. Martin Luther's Vermischte Deutsche Schriften*, ed. Johann K. Irmischer, vol. 63 (Erlangen: Heyder and Zimmer, 1854), pp. 124-25, August 1994, http://www.iclnet.org/pub/resources/text/wittenberg/luther/luther-faith.txt: italics added.

16   Mt 7:17-20.

Chapter 9

1 "White Man's Burden," Answers.com, http://www.answers.com/topic/the-white-man-s-burden#Differing_interpretations.

2 There were many noteworthy exceptions to this. A third of the German Church became the "confessing church" and were willing to suffer in many instances martyrdom—Dietrich Bonhoeffer being a well known example.

3 "Christian Terrorism," Wikipedia (last modified January 30, 2011), http://en.wikipedia.org/wiki/Christian_Terrorism.

4 Paul-Gordon Chandler, *Pilgrims of Christ on the Muslim Road*, (Lanham, MD: Cowley Publications, 2007), p. 109.

5 John J. Travis and J. Dudley Woodberry, "When God's Kingdom Grows Like Yeast: Frequently-Asked Questions within Muslim Communities," *Mission Frontiers* (The U.S. Center for World Missions) 32:4, July-August 2010, pp. 26-27.

6 Chandler, *Pilgrims of Christ on the Muslim Road*, p. 18.

7 Mt 22:16-22; Mk 12:13-17.

8 This is a personal paraphrase of 1 Cor 7:18-24.

9 Gal 2:11-16.

10 For example, the International Council of Ethnodoxologists (ICE).

11 E. Stanley Jones, *The Christ of the Indian Road* (New York: Abingdon, 1925), p. 12.

12 Ibid., pp. 27-28.

13 Dibin Samuel, "Mahatma Gandhi and Christianity" (Christian Today, copyright Christian Today India 2002-20080, http://in.christiantoday.com/articledir/print.htm?id=2837.

14 Rick Wood, "Editorial Comment," *Mission Frontiers* (The U.S. Center for World Missions) 32:5, September-October 2010, pp. 4-5.

15 Dot Everett, "The Sweat Lodge: Can God Use It?" *Mission Frontiers* (The U.S. Center for World Missions) 32:5, September-October 2010, p. 10.

16 Chandler, *Pilgrims of Christ on the Muslim Road*, p. 104.

17 Jn 4:6-30; Mt 8:5-13.

18 Lk 3:14.

19 Ralph D. Winter, "Learn From Our Mistakes," *Mission Frontiers* (The U.S. Center for World Missions) 34:3, May-June 2012, pp. 18-21.

20 Mark D. Siljander, *A Deadly Misunderstanding: A Congressman's Quest to Bridge the Muslim-Christian Divide* (New York: HarperCollins, 2008), pp. 153-54.

21 A good book on lifting up Jesus and not promoting "Christianity" is Carl Medearis, *Speaking of Jesus* (Colorado Springs, CO: David C. Cook, 2011).

22 Jn 12:32.

23 Wikipedia describes "Christianization" as "the practice of converting native pagan practices and culture" sometimes by force (http://en.wikipedia.org/wiki/Christianization; last modified December 29, 2010).

Chapter 10

1 The actual words were "Houston, we've a problem."

2 Jn 3:16-18, italics added.

3 Acts 4:12 MSG; see also 1 Jn 2:22-23.

4 1 Tim 2:5.

5 1 Cor 1:23-24.

6 C. S. Lewis, *Mere Christianity* (London: Fontana Books, 1952), p. 52.

7 Michael R. Licona, in William A. Dembski and Michael R.

Licona, eds., *Evidence for God* (Grand Rapids, MI: Baker Books, 2010), p. 198.

8   Acts 17:30; see also Jn 15:22.

9   Mt 16: 13; Mk 8:27.

10   Mt 16:13-16; Mk 8:27-29.

11   Jn 20:28. The evidence for the deity of Christ is very strong in the Scriptures. Revelation 19:16 describes him as King of Kings and Lord of Lords. He creates (Jn 1:2-3; Col 1:16) and he accepts worship. (Mt 14:33; Heb 1:6-8).

12   Erwin W. Lutzer, *Your Eternal Reward* (Chicago: Moody Press, 1998), pp. 166-67. Ron Rhodes says, "God always judges people according to the light given." *Heaven: The Undiscovered Country* (Eugene, OR: Harvest House, 1996), p. 133.

13   Some verses on our personal need; that we don't measure up to God's standards: Rom 3:23; 6:23.

14   Some verses indicating that access is only through Christ: Mt 7:13-23; Lk 10:16; Jn 1:17; 3:16-18, 36; 5:24; 10:9-10; 14:6-9; 17:3; 18:37; Acts 4:12; 16:30-31; Rom 1:16; 10:9-13; 1 Cor 1:22-24; 1 Tim 1:15; 2:5; Heb 1:1-3; 9:12; 1 Jn 2:1-2, 23; 5:1-3, 11-13.

15   Some verses indicating that Christ was born, lived a sinless life, was crucified, died, arose from the dead, and has ascended into heaven: Jn 1:14; Acts 2:22-36; 1 Cor 15:2-8; 1 Thess 4:14; Heb 1:3; 1 Pet 1:3-5, 18-19.

16   Some passages mandating repentance (Mt 3:2; 4:17; Mk 1:15; 6:12; Lk 13:3-5; Acts 2:38; 3:19; 17:30) and others indicating that our life should manifest our faith: Rom 10:9-10; 1 Jn 3:3-24; 4:7-8. See my entire chapter 8. (Note: Throughout Christian history baptism has been an extremely important issue; however, I do not believe the Bible teaches that baptism is *essential* for salvation. The Bible does say that the one who believes and is baptized is saved (Mk 16:16). However, this passage is not in the

original manuscripts. I believe baptism is a normal part of the external manifestations of a life in Christ and generally believers will want to identify with Christ in baptism, but it is not an essential requirement for salvation. The thief on the cross was not baptized yet clearly was saved. No passage in the Bible says that if you are not baptized you will not go to heaven. Baptism is one of *many* ways to express identification with Christ.)

17   Acts 4:12; Rom 10:9-10; 1 Tim 2:5.

18   1 Tim 2:3-6.

19   Jer 29:13-14, Mt 7:7-8; Lk 11:9; Jn 18:37; Acts 17:27; 18:24-28.

20   John Sanders, *No Other Name: An Investigation into the Destiny of the Unevangelized* (Eugene, OR: Wipf and Stock, 2001), p. 154. See also Jn 8:41-47, 56; Acts 4:12; 10:1-48; 18:24-28; Rom 5:17-19.

21   Edith Schaeffer, *Affliction: A Compassionate Look at the Reality of Pain and Suffering* (Grand Rapids, MI: Baker Books, 1978, 1993), p. 125.

Chapter 11

1   *It seems to me* a major reason for many to oppose the idea that individuals today can be saved through general revelation is the effect that such an idea might have on missions. For example John Piper, in *Jesus: The Only Way to God; Must You Hear the Gospel to Be Saved?* (Grand Rapids, MI: Baker Books, 2010), expresses several times and summarizes on page 122, "So I affirm again that the abandonment of the universal necessity of hearing the gospel for salvation does indeed diminish the urgency of world evangelization." I wholeheartedly concur with the concern for missions but believe we must be careful not to allow this to color what the Scriptures may in fact say about general revelation.

2   There is no evidence that any of these had specific or special

revelation prior to their deep faith in God. With their obedience to general revelation God sent more truth.

3   There is considerable debate as to whether few or many might be saved through this means. Three verses have been used to suggest only few will be saved by general revelation: Mt 7:14; 22:14; Lk 13:23-24. See Terrance L. Tiessen, *Who Can Be Saved? Reassessing Salvation in Christ and World Religions* (Downers Grove, IL: InterVarsity Press, 2004), p. 289.

4   The Scriptures, in all four Gospels and the book of Acts, clearly command us to send ambassadors throughout the world; see Mt 28:18-20; Mk 13:10; 16:15-16; Lk 24:47-48; Jn 20:21; Acts 1:8.

5   See Sir Norman Anderson, *Christianity and World Religions* (Leicester, England: Inter-Varsity Press, 1970, 1984), pp. 154-55 for further comments on this issue.

6   "Sati," Wikipedia, http://en.wikipedia.org/wiki/Sati_(practice), (last modified 9/15/11).

7   Lamin Sanneh, *Translating the Message: The Missionary Impact on Culture* (Maryknoll, New York, 2009).

8   Matthew D. LaPlante, "Ethiopia's River of Death," *Christianity Today,* August 2011, pp. 40-44.

9   E. Stanley Jones, *The Christ of the Indian Road* (New York: Abingdon, 1925), p. 118.

10 Paul-Gordon Chandler, *Pilgrims of Christ on the Muslim Road* (Lanham, MD: Cowley Publications, 2007), p. 23.

11 Mt 23:13 NET.

12 Jones, *Christ of the Indian Road*, p. 22.

13 Followers of Christ are referred to as "Christians" in Acts 11:26; 26:28 and 1 Pet 4:16, and as followers of "the Way" in Acts 9:2; 19:9, 23; 24:14, 22.

14 Chandler, *Pilgrims of Christ on the Muslim Road*, p. 79.

15 Tim Stafford, "India's Grassroots Revival," *Christianity Today*, July 8, 2011, p. 2, http://christianitytoday.com/ct/article_print .html?id=92825.

Afterword

1   1 Cor 9:24; Heb 12:1-3; see also 1 Cor 9:26; 1 Tim 6:12; 2 Tim 4:7-8.

2   Erwin W. Lutzer, *Your Eternal Reward* (Chicago: Moody Press, 1998), p. 21, italics in original.

3   *Iran: Desperate for God*, produced by The Voice of the Martyrs, author not given (Bartlesville, OK: Living Sacrifice Book Company, 2008), p. 126.

4   Rep. Paul Broun Jr., MD, Personal Testimony, *Christian Doctor's Digest* 13, no. 2, tract 4, April 2008, P.O. Box 7500, Bristol, TN.

5   1 Chr 28:9: "If you seek Him, He will be found by you, but if you forsake Him, He will cast you off forever." Isa 55:6: "Seek the Lord while He may be found, Call upon Him while He is near." Jer 29:13-14a: "you will seek Me and find Me when you search for Me with all your heart." Jn 5:39: "Search the Scriptures for in them you think you have eternal life; and these are they which testify of me."

6   Dallas Willard, *Renovation of the Heart* (Colorado Springs, CO: NavPress, 2002), p. 149.

7   In a private communication with the Billy Graham Evangelistic Association they verified that Billy Graham did share the Einstein story at the United Nations in December 1999, but regarding the suit story, they said, "He could have shared the suit story as well at some point, but we have not been able to confirm it."

8   "This World Is Not My Home," words and music by Albert E. Brumley, © 1965- Albert E. Brumley & Sons.

9   1 John 5:13 RSV.